Improving the Visibility and Use of Digital Repositories through SEO

AF764080

ALA TechSource purchases fund advocacy, awareness, and accreditation programs for library professionals worldwide.

lita

Improving the Visibility and Use of Digital Repositories through SEO

A LITA Guide

Kenning Arlitsch
and
Patrick S. OBrien

ALA TechSource

An imprint of the American Library Association

CHICAGO 2013

© 2013 by the American Library Association. Any claim of copyright is subject to applicable limitations and exceptions, such as rights of fair use and library copying pursuant to Sections 107 and 108 of the U.S. Copyright Act. No copyright is claimed for content in the public domain, such as works of the U.S. government.

Printed in the United States of America

17 16 15 14 13 5 4 3 2 1

Extensive effort has gone into ensuring the reliability of the information in this book; however, the publisher makes no warranty, express or implied, with respect to the material contained herein.

ISBNs: 978-1-55570-906-8 (paper); 978-1-55570-924-2 (PDF). For more information on digital formats, visit the ALA Store at alastore.ala.org and select eEditions.

Library of Congress Cataloging-in-Publication Data

Arlitsch, Kenning.

Improving the visibility and use of digital repositories through SEO / Kenning Arlitsch and Patrick S. OBrien.

pages cm. — (LITA guides)

Includes bibliographical references and index.

ISBN 978-1-55570-906-8 (alk. paper)

1. Library Web sites—Design. 2. Library Web sites—Statistical methods. 3. Web search engines. 4. Electronic information resources—Management. 5. Digital libraries. 6. Institutional repositories. 7. Libraries and the Internet. 8. Webliometrics. I. O'Brien, Patrick (Patrick S.) II. Title.

Z674.75.W67A75 2013

025.0422—dc23 2012049197

Book design in Berkeley and Avenir. Cover image ©Shutterstock, Inc.

∞ This paper meets the requirements of ANSI/NISO Z39.48-1992 (Permanence of Paper).

Contents

Preface

Search engine optimization (SEO) has become a common term in the vocabulary of the Internet. We all want to get our websites and other web publications included in search engine indexes, because those engines are arguably the most important discovery tools for our potential users. Much has been published about the practice of SEO on websites, blogs, journals, and books, and there is very good information available in many of those outlets that can be applied to general websites. But very little has been written about SEO for digital repositories, and they are different.

Libraries and archives have made enormous investments in creating digital collections for more than a decade, and many simply expected search engines to find those digital objects and include them in their indexes. The reality, unfortunately, is that the success rate of repository-based digital objects appearing in search engine indexes is quite low. Creating a successful SEO strategy is a process of raising awareness, setting goals, developing new skill sets, communicating across the organization, and continuous monitoring. There are, of course, technical aspects, but as we stress in this book, SEO is not the exclusive domain of an organization's information technology (IT) department. Making print collections available to users has always been an organization-wide responsibility, with numerous departments and individuals making contributions to the collection's goals, organization, visibility, and use. Making digital collections available is no different.

Search engines like Google, Bing, Yahoo!, and others whose mission it is to index the contents of the Web have set themselves an incredibly complex task. *Daunting* is a word we use later in this book, but even that term is inadequate. Think about it this way: a 2011 estimate put the size of the Web at well over one trillion unique URLs, and over 555 million websites and growing. The competition is fierce, and major search engines come nowhere close to indexing all those URLs and sites. Yet, not only do we want our digital library objects to appear in search engine indexes, but we also want them to appear on the first or second pages of search results because we know that most users don't venture much beyond those initial pages. Given the enormous and dynamic environment that is the Web, search engines do an incredible job by writing crawling and indexing programs that use sophisticated algorithms. But search engines can't do it all themselves—they need all the help we can give them.

Libraries and archives have an honored tradition of service to our users, but the definition of those users has changed in the age of the Internet. Our users, or at least our mediators to users, are now machines, and machines have different information needs than humans. They don't understand context, nuance, and colloquialisms—at least not yet. Machines require highly structured data, with definitions established at the outset. Optimizing metadata for machines is not a difficult process, but it does require a different mindset, and there are enormous opportunities for catalogers in this changed paradigm.

Another change in the paradigm is realizing that our users don't become "ours" until they reach our websites. While they work with the search engines that we hope will connect them to us, they are "customers" of the search engines, and search engines are businesses that want to deliver a good product. The business wants to know if you are worthy of their customers. Do you have a good product that you can be trusted to deliver quickly and efficiently when the search engine's customer asks for it? Is it accurately described and is it of good quality? These are factors that are weighed by search engines as they determine whether to include your product in their inventory and how high that product will appear in their rankings.

We have written from a broad perspective and painstakingly provided endnotes with references to the sources we recommend readers to use to learn more about implementing the ideas and concepts presented. We hope this book will be useful to people in a variety of positions in libraries and archives. Yes, there is quite a bit of technical detail in some of the chapters that is aimed specifically at IT professionals. But there is also enough general overview that is useful to administrators who will benefit enormously from the visibility that proper SEO can bring to an organization, as well as hard statistics and reports they can use to demonstrate the value the library or archive brings to its parent institution and the communities it serves. There is also good information for archivists or collection managers, or other stakeholders who have an interest in making the digital version of their collections more accessible and useful.

The users are out there. This book will help bring them to you.

Chapter One

What Is SEO and Why Is It Important to Libraries?

Search engine optimization (SEO) is the practice of assuring that websites are indexed and effectively presented in Internet search results. Internet search engines drive enormous amounts of traffic to websites, and the sites that can't easily be found through a major search engine will usually suffer from a lack of visitation. How crucial is this point? A 2005 survey conducted by OCLC demonstrated that 89 percent of college students began their research with Internet search engines, and that only 2 percent began at library websites (De Rosa et al. 2005). A 2010 update to the study showed that the situation for library websites had deteriorated, with "not a single survey respondent [reporting that they] began their information search on a library website" (De Rosa et al. 2011). Despite more than a decade of library instruction programs that point out the lack of credibility and accuracy of some of the information found through search engines, students continue to search in the way that's easiest and most convenient for them.

It's not only students who ignore library websites and go straight to Internet search engines to begin their research. A 2010 study of active faculty researchers at four major universities discovered that "researchers find Google and Google Scholar to be amazingly effective" for their information retrieval needs and accept the results as "good enough in many cases" (Kroll, Forsman, and OCLC Research 2010). The 2009 Ithaka Faculty Survey found that "discovery through Google and Google Scholar is in a third-place position, virtually tied with a variety of other discovery practices" (Schonfeld and Housewright 2010).

Students and faculty are crucial constituents for academic libraries, but donors and funding agencies are another important population that should be considered in the SEO landscape. Donors contribute money or their valuable archival materials, and they use search engines just like anyone else. Donors were an early driver of our SEO research, because at one point we found ourselves in the unfortunate position of some donors being unable find the collections they had contributed via search engines, even though we had digitized the collections and loaded them into our repository. Unhappy donors tend to stop contributing, but fortunately we were able to address the problem in time. Public funding agencies want to be assured that the taxpayer monies they are devoting to a given project will have broad reach, and in the SEO context this means being able to demonstrate that users are finding and using the digital collections being created with grant funding.

These examples are meant to drive home a point: if the objects that a library has digitized do not appear in Internet search engine indexes, they will not be found by the majority of potential users. It's hard to demonstrate a positive return on investment when the use of digital repositories is low. Conversely, we have demonstrated conclusively that increasing our visibility in Internet search engines (see figure 1.1) leads to increased visitation (see figure 1.2).

Another important point we would like to make right from the start is that SEO is not purely a technical problem. Of course there are a lot of technical issues involved and we'll certainly discuss those, but SEO cannot succeed if it's thought of as being a problem of the IT department. SEO is really about connecting users

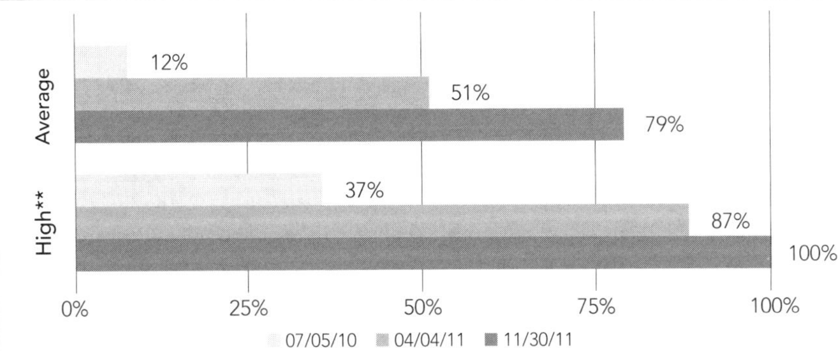

* Google Index Ratio = URLs submitted / URLs Indexed by Google for about 150 collections containing ~170,000 URLs

** Highest index ratio achieved for Collections with over 500 URLs submitted to Google

FIGURE 1.1

Google Index Ratios—All Collections*

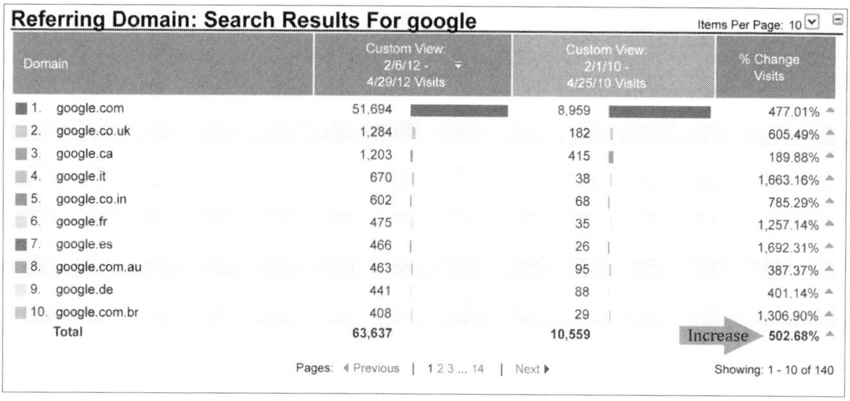

Referring Domain: Search Results For google — Items Per Page: 10

Domain	Custom View: 2/6/12 - 4/29/12 Visits	Custom View: 2/1/10 - 4/25/10 Visits	% Change Visits
1. google.com	51,694	8,959	477.01%
2. google.co.uk	1,284	182	605.49%
3. google.ca	1,203	415	189.88%
4. google.it	670	38	1,663.16%
5. google.co.in	602	68	785.29%
6. google.fr	475	35	1,257.14%
7. google.es	466	26	1,692.31%
8. google.com.au	463	95	387.37%
9. google.de	441	88	401.14%
10. google.com.br	408	29	1,306.90%
Total	63,637	10,559	Increase 502.68%

Pages: ◂ Previous | 1 2 3 ... 14 | Next ▸ Showing: 1 - 10 of 140

FIGURE 1.2
Google Traffic Increase

to information, and just as everyone who worked with print collections carried that philosophy of service, everyone in the organization now must take some responsibility for continuing to make digital information available to users. You might think we're kidding when we say this, but we're not. Administrators, archivists, catalogers, reference and instruction librarians, and yes, IT personnel all play important roles in this new world. Above all, SEO is about understanding what the organization is trying to achieve and communicating across multiple departments to make sure everyone is informed and involved.

WEBSITES VS. REPOSITORIES

While we used the term *websites* freely in our introduction, this book is only peripherally about SEO for library websites, because that subject has been written about extensively. There are numerous books, blogs, and websites that deal with general SEO, many of them focusing on businesses and how they can better connect customers to their products. There's a lot of good information in many of those sources, and some of it applies to libraries and archives. Much less has been written specifically about SEO for digital repositories, the databases that contain digitized or born-digital objects that libraries and archives have been creating and making available to the public largely free of charge for more than a decade. These repositories offer cultural heritage collections digitized from various formats of materials, including photographs, documents, maps, newspapers, books, and audio and video files. Some, like institutional repositories, have sought to change traditional publishing models by promoting open access philosophies and trying to ensure that the published products of taxpayer-funded research remain freely accessible, in perpetuity. Data sets are an increasingly important aspect of digital libraries, as librarians engage with researchers to help them organize and manage the data upon which the conclusions of their research depend. With substantial help from government and private granting agencies, and from donors, libraries have poured many millions of dollars into the creation and maintenance of these repositories, and making sure that potential users can find them is a crucial part of the process.

Libraries usually develop introductory websites that act as portals to the thousands or even millions of individual objects contained in their repositories, and for years we expected that users would find the objects through those portals. But users rarely behave the way we want them to; they'll do what's in their own best discovery interest. Nine times out of ten, as the OCLC studies show, users will begin their research with search engines, and they will link directly to the digital objects they find there, rather than go through the browse or search mechanisms offered on our local websites.

Our history with creating digital repositories at the University of Utah stretches back to the turn of the century, and over the following decade we amassed a considerable collection of objects that our partners or we had digitized. With well over one million digitized newspaper pages and nearly half a million digital objects of every other format, we were proud of what we had achieved. At first, we didn't worry much about whether our digital objects were being harvested and indexed by search engines—we just assumed that they were. A few years ago some doubt began to creep into that assumption as staff began to notice that, more often than not, they couldn't find our digital objects in Google, and after some more investigation we began to understand just how bad the problem really was. We decided to put some benchmarks into place, and found that our average digital collections indexing ratio in Google hovered somewhere around 12 percent in July 2010 (we'll explain "indexing ratio" in detail in chapter 5). Naturally, we worried that we might be the only library having these problems, so in October, our budding SEO team conducted a randomized survey of 650 known digital objects in thirteen repositories of the Mountain West Digital Library (MWDL). The survey revealed a disturbing pattern: only 38 percent of digital objects searched by title were found in Google's main index. Worse, this Google search engine results page (SERP) consisted mainly of links back to sets of search results in the local repositories, rather than linking directly to the objects. We called these "indirect links" (see figure 1.3), and when we removed those from survey results we found that only 15 percent of the hits on the SERP provided users with direct links to the objects (see figure 1.4). The known-item title searching method that we employed probably produced the best results possible at the time; searching by keyword or subject term would likely have retrieved even fewer items from the digital collections represented in the MWDL.

In subsequent, informal searches of other repositories we found results similar to the MWDL survey. Some repositories performed better, while others had even lower visibility. Some institutional repositories had good showings in Google, but not in Google Scholar. Most general-purpose repositories (digital collections) that we surveyed had almost no presence in Google Images. Based on presentations we have given around the country and conversations with colleagues, it is apparent that most libraries are unaware how poorly their repositories perform in search engines, and their staffs generally lack the knowledge and skills to implement effective SEO practices.

FIGURE 1.3
Indirect URL

FIGURE 1.4
Direct URL

SUPPORTING LIBRARIES' VALUE PROPOSITION

As the economic recession that began in 2008 tightened budgets, more emphasis was being placed on assessment and measurement of outputs. Researchers who make their data sets available to support their publications have been shown to enjoy an increased rate of citations (Piwowar, Day, and Fridsma 2007). Other research in the United Kingdom (Key Perspectives Ltd. and Brown 2009) suggests that institutional repositories (IR) might play a crucial role in measuring research output, and in turn might affect university rankings. The *Times Higher Education* publishes an annual ranking of the top world universities in which author citations contribute 32.5 percent toward each university's score (Baty 2011). A comparison of Web of Science, Scopus, and Google Scholar as sources for citation analysis and researcher ranking concluded that while Google Scholar was still deficient (in 2006) in its indexing of journal articles it nonetheless stood out "in its coverage of conference proceedings as well as international, non-English journals, among others" as well as indexing "a wide variety of document types" (Meho and Yang 2007). Use of Google Scholar has only increased since that study was published, but as we will demonstrate in chapter 7 it has significant problems crawling and indexing IR. Academic libraries have led the open access movement and the development of IR. But just as IRs are gaining enough mass to make them useful and credible sources of research output, the difficulties associated with SEO threaten to undermine their potential.

RESEARCH RESULTS AT UTAH

Since assessing the scope of the problem in 2010 we have been actively working to improve the visibility of the University of Utah's repositories in search engines, and we have had great success. We will explain our strategies in following chapters, but for now we'll list several general challenges that affect how well a repository will be represented in a search engine's index.

- Web servers may not be configured correctly to invite search engine crawlers, and server speed performance may be unacceptably slow.
- Metadata are often not unique or structured as recognizable ontologies, and in some cases search engines may not accept the schema employed by the repository.
- Repository software may present an impenetrable labyrinth for crawlers.
- Search engine policies and practices change and must be monitored accordingly.
- Search engines may not support accepted standards and protocols in the library community (such as OAI-PMH).

SEARCH ENGINES

There are many search engines that showed great promise in the early days of the Internet that have diminished or disappeared altogether. Remember Alta Vista? Ask Jeeves? DogPile? Google has risen to the top and demonstrated staying power over the past decade, consistently garnering about 66 percent of the direct search engine market share in the United States (comScore 2012). Despite a strong effort by Microsoft's Bing search engine, which also powers Yahoo!'s search, Google shows no signs of surrendering its place; its market share has remained steady for the two years that we've been tracking it. It is important to note that the Google and Bing indexes are separate and have different rules for harvesting and indexing. While the practices we offer in this book can be applied to most search engines, we will focus primarily on Google and Google Scholar.

Search engines can be thought of as "users with substantial constraints: they can't read text in images, can't interpret JavaScript or applets, and can't 'view' many other kinds of multimedia content" (Hagans 2005). Search engines need help in understanding what they're "seeing," and that means libraries and archives should create machine-readable metadata and give them useful on-page text to index. Google and other search engines encourage adherence to W3C web content accessibility guidelines, a clearly defined standard to which libraries should aspire for ethical reasons (helping visually disabled users) as well as improving SEO.

Standards and Protocols

Librarians and archivists are great believers in standards, and while building digital repositories they have respected and even helped develop standards for digital imaging, metadata, harvesting, and web services, among others. Unfortunately, search engines are not required to honor those standards. The following two examples demonstrate the impotence of library standards in the search engine world:

In 2008 Google announced discontinuation of support for OAI-PMH, the metadata harvesting protocol that has been widely adopted by libraries (Mueller 2008).

In August 2010, Google Scholar made the following announcement on its Webmaster Inclusion Guidelines site: "Use Dublin Core tags (e.g., DC.title) as a last resort—they work poorly for journal papers" (Google Scholar 2011a).

Whereas repository managers may have correctly presumed they were being indexed more fully prior to the OAI-PMH change, many we spoke with were not aware of the announcement or the purging effect the change may have had on their repositories' presence in Google's indexes. The announcement about Dublin Core metadata was even more disconcerting, since most libraries' digital repositories use it to describe their collections. Instead of Dublin Core, Google Scholar recommends using other schemas, such as Highwire Press, Eprints, bepress, and PRISM (more on this in chapter 7). Many librarians despair that they must now manually change their IR metadata schema to assure inclusion in Google Scholar. Part of our research includes developing solutions to help transform metadata schemas when it is prudent and necessary.

Social Media Engines

Another kind of search engine is also beginning to make its presence known. Facebook's Open Graph protocol brings an entirely new dimension, powering "a social search—one based on likes instead of links" (Ingram 2010). In 2010, Facebook surpassed Google for total share of Internet traffic for the first time (McGee 2010b). Not one to be left behind, Google recently introduced a new indexing system known as Caffeine, which places more emphasis on content that is continually being refreshed and updated, like blogs and social media sites (Grimes 2010). As the content in library and archive digital repositories tends to be static, this new emphasis presents an additional challenge. Later on in this book we will talk about developing communities that can help make repositories known through social media venues.

BLACK HATS AND WHITE HATS

Businesses have long practiced SEO as a way of connecting customers to their products, and much has been written about that intensely competitive environment. Search engines are notoriously secretive about exactly how their algorithms work, and efforts to fool or "game" them into increased indexing or higher results rankings have been met with penalties that include temporary demotions in search engine results, or even outright removal from the search engine's indexes. These "black hat" techniques are to be avoided at all cost.

"White hat" SEO techniques are those that are viewed by Google and other search engines as legitimate and acceptable efforts to become visible in search engine results. White hat techniques adhere to the guidelines and suggestions posted by search engines on various "webmaster tools" sites (Google 2010; Bing 2009). Generally speaking, if search engines suggest a particular practice or policy for your repository it is best to follow those suggestions completely. Chapter 6 will provide specific recommendations for legitimately structuring the content of digital repositories for improved access and use.

The Case of J.C. Penney

In 2010 J.C. Penney's SEO consulting firm used "link schemes" to raise product visibility in Google's search results. In simple terms, they seeded unrelated websites around the world with references to J.C. Penney products. It worked stupendously for a while, until the *New York Times* investigated why Penney was beating out so many other retailers and then reported their findings to Google. Google quickly determined that the practices were "black hat" and took "corrective action" (Segal 2011). Within days, J.C. Penney dropped almost out of sight in the SERP.

SUMMARY

The importance of SEO to digital repositories in libraries and archives cannot be underestimated. At a time when these organizations are increasingly being asked to demonstrate their value proposition, SEO can help bring more students, faculty, and other users to the digital collections offered by a library or an archive. It may also help raise university rankings by increasing research citation rates.

The search engine landscape is dynamic and competitive, and getting indexed successfully by a search engine requires consistent monitoring to keep up with developments and policy changes. Getting indexed doesn't mean that the job is done, because the next crawl conducted by the harvester could result in digital objects being expelled from an index, for a variety of reasons that we will explain. There are legitimate and recommended ways to conduct SEO, and there are techniques that could result in damage to your SEO efforts.

Chapter 2 will focus on the organizational roles and communication required for successful SEO. It's written from a management perspective, to give a high-level administrator an understanding of all the pieces and the people that are required to practice SEO and improve online visitation. Although it's written from that perspective, other staff will recognize their roles and perhaps glean some new information about their relationship to the work ahead. From an organizational standpoint, this may well be the most important chapter in this book.

Chapter Two

Improving Your Library's SEO Efforts

The practice of search engine optimization is not the domain of one individual or department. SEO is most effective when it is a consideration and is "owned" by multiple people across several departments. Just as it takes many people to make print collections accessible to the public, SEO practiced broadly will help ensure that items in the digital library will be accessible as well. Some SEO solutions are technical in nature, but others are not. Whether technical or administrative, they all require communication, management, and coordination to ensure that people are working together to achieve common goals. Most important, the effective practice of SEO requires direction from the organization's leadership, which will use statistics and data gathered from SEO analysis tools to make course corrections and to help communicate a narrative about what the library is trying to achieve for its users. This chapter is written from an organizational perspective and is primarily aimed at higher-level administrators, but that doesn't mean you systems administrators will not get anything out of it.

WHERE SEO IS NEEDED IN LIBRARIES

Search engines index digital files and their metadata, and therefore SEO is naturally considered to be the concern of people who manage technology. While it is true that effective SEO addresses the layers of technology that manage and deliver digital content, it's good to remember that those technologies are simply tools that serve the needs of people, and not just IT people. SEO really is the concern of anyone whose work is represented on the Internet because it impacts how accessible that work is to the intended audience. If this book makes only one impression on the reader, it should be to realize that SEO is not something that should be left exclusively to an organization's IT department: "an IT department should not be left to make, often by default, the choices that determine the impact of IT on a company's business strategy"(Ross and Weill 2002). Nearly every employee has some interest or influence in the content and the services that a library makes available on the Web, and that makes for many stakeholders. Both technology and people should be driven by the goals of the organization.

> We often use the vocabulary of the academic library because that's the environment we work in and know best. Other types of libraries have their own vocabularies to describe their users and reporting structures.

SETTING EXPECTATIONS AND USING METRICS

Statistics have long been a part of our business. Libraries have always counted the size of their collections—the number of items borrowed, interlibrary loans, expenditures—and we have always used those numbers to create comparisons to other libraries. SEO continues this tradition of measurement, with additional complexity and some variation in the vocabulary. Gate counts for physical visits are still needed, but counting online visitors is at least as important, and can actually tell us a whole lot more about our users (in anonymous terms) than traditional counts can.

The "currencies" that sustain a library's digital repositories are grants, partnerships, and donations of money and collections. To demonstrate their value and to make a case for an influx of these currencies, libraries need to move beyond counting basic page views and visits to individual websites. They must break down silos and look at the entire user click stream across all their web properties to create metrics their internal and external stakeholders value. This is an important concept: it's not enough to track user behavior on a single web server because that almost certainly provides only a partial picture. One server may contain the library's website, another server hosts a digital repository, and a third may serve streaming video to users. A single machine can also host multiple web servers. While they are probably all in the organization's domain, tools and structures should be set up appropriately to track users as they move from one server to another.

Institutional repositories may increase academic participation if they provide metrics and services tailored for individual academic authors, department heads, and college deans. For example, a library can provide to each department and college a dashboard that might contain the following metrics:

- Number of publications indexed by Google
- Page Views
- Total Visits
- PDF Downloads
- Bibliographic Citation Downloads

A similar dashboard for each digital collection could help the library's leadership team have discussions with current and future donors, as well as help collection managers who want to demonstrate value to grant providers and collaboration partners. These metrics provide objective data that support a dialogue with the university's academic administration about the value of the IR and how individual academics, departments, and colleges can better utilize it.

ROLES AND RESPONSIBILITIES

Libraries and archives differ in mission and size, and those factors shape their organizational structures. Whether the organization is flat or has a hierarchy that supports several levels is somewhat irrelevant for our purposes. Every organization that creates and manages digital repositories, or outsources that work, requires feedback about those repositories, and therefore many people in those organizations can be said to have SEO roles.

Author citation rates are positively correlated with the availability and ease of access to the paper's full-text content. We believe that the sooner the full text of an academic paper housed in an open-access IR is indexed by search engines, the more likely it will be found and cited. We hope researchers use data captured from IR web server logs to test linkages between the IR, academic citations, and academic funding.

Administrators

Administrators are the leadership team of the library or archive, and their specific positions carry titles like dean, director, or university librarian, and associate dean/director or associate university librarian. This team develops long-term strategies and short-term goals, often with input from the rest of the organization, and it is the administrators who are most often called upon to report the state of the library and its initiatives. A library director may report to her provost, city council, board of directors, accrediting agency, a conference of peers, or to the staff of the library. Reporting is enhanced by data, and numbers that tell a story about the library's performance will help administrators. The SEO role of the library administrator is to require metrics from his or her staff that will help clarify their story. Administrators should analyze those metrics and ask if the library's goals are being met, and if not, why not? In figure 2.1 we have overlaid common SEO risk areas on typical digital repository roles and provided some suggestions about each role's responsibility for managing the SEO risk. Administrators should maintain an awareness of these issues and set expectations with their staff about each risk area.

Collection Managers

Collection managers are most familiar with the content of a given collection. They may be archivists or librarians, and the technology issues concerning the digital version of the collection are often of secondary interest. They care deeply for the collection itself, and they are intensely interested in how that collection is described and presented. They want to know how the collection is being used, whether in its analog or digital version. The SEO role of the collection manager is similar to a product-marketing manager with a great deal of responsibility for promoting the product, that is, the digital collection in question. They know who the target audiences are and why they might value the collection. They play a critical role in establishing the collection's goals (i.e., downloads, inquiries, referrals, and so on) and ensuring the written content in the repository incorporates keywords focused on communicating the collection's purpose, contents, and value to the appropriate audiences. They also have the knowledge needed for "off-page" SEO, including knowing the community leaders who share an interest in increasing awareness of the collection and are likely to offer support by linking to it from their websites, blogs, Facebook pages, and so on. The collection manager will know what internal and external links a user might find useful when visiting a page within their collection. These "off-page" signals are used by search engines to rank the trust, context, authority, and value of a website for a user they might refer. In figure 2.1 we have included common SEO risk areas for which collection managers should take responsibility and the support roles they will need. We have also included information on which roles should have accountability to the collection manager in addressing their collection's SEO risks. Collection managers may be called upon to produce reports for administrators and the collection's other stakeholders.

IT Personnel

IT departments vary greatly in size, and some libraries and archives don't have them at all and outsource their needs to campus or commercial entities. Libraries that rely on external organizations for IT services should ensure those providers have the necessary services in place that support collection mangers' and administrators' SEO efforts.

IT Managers

Those with robust internal IT departments may feel they have more control of their destinies, but they may also have a significant education and management task ahead because chances that any significant SEO expertise already exists among staff are low. IT departments may deal with such diverse areas as desktop computing, digitization, website development and management, intranet, programming, integrated library systems and discovery layers, systems hardware, file storage, and digital preservation. Many of these functions have a direct impact on SEO. The SEO role of the IT manager is to know how all these pieces work in conjunction to affect SEO, how to deliver the services that are useful to administrators and collection managers, and to ensure that IT staff are educated and communicating with each other about the changes they make to their systems.

Systems Administrators

Systems administrators are typically responsible for the web server layer containing the digital collection's hardware, operating system (OS), and web server. They must have a good understanding of what search engine crawlers are looking for, and configure their web servers accordingly. They need to know how to minimize barriers to those crawlers in the web server software (e.g., Apache or Microsoft IIS are the most common) and the web application software packages that are installed on top of that web server. Figure 2.1 contains a number of SEO risks related to the web server layer that systems administrators will likely encounter and the other

Risk Area: Web Server	Chapter	Adminis-trator	Collection Manager	Cataloger	IT Manager
5XX and 4XX HTTP errors	4, 5	Awareness			Responsible
Redirects and rewrites (HTTP 301 & 302)	4, 5		Responsible		Awareness
Domain alias	4, 5				Responsible
Server performance tuning	5	Awareness			Awareness
Robots.txt	3				Awareness
Sitemaps	3		Responsible		Awareness
Risk Area: Application Layer					
URL structure	4, 5				Awareness
JavaScript	5				Awareness
Multiple URLs for identical content	5	Awareness			Awareness
Risk Area: Presentation Layer					
HTML errors	5				Awareness
HTML page structure	6	Awareness	Responsible		Awareness
Incorrect or nonexistent "machine readable" micro tagging	6, 7	Awareness	Responsible		Awareness
Undeclared standards, schemas, or taxonomies	6, 7		Awareness		Responsible
Internal link structure	4	Awareness	Support		Awareness
Incorrect or incomplete analytics page code	4, 8	Awareness			Responsible
Risk Area: Metadata					
Key word choices	6, 8	Awareness	Responsible	Support	
Nonexistent, redundant, or generalized descriptive metadata	6, 8	Awareness	Responsible	Accountable	
Undefined or inconsistent application of taxonomies / vocabularies—using vocabulary that is unique to the organization.	6	Awareness	Responsible	Accountable	
Incorrect or nonexistent use of micro tagging—putting all citation elements in a single field.	6, 7	Awareness	Responsible	Accountable	
Inconsistent or nonconformance with known standards or Search Engine policies	3, 4, 5, 7				Responsible
Inconsistent quality, e.g., spelling of names, logical relationships, syntax	6, 7, 8	Awareness	Responsible	Accountable	

Awareness: Ensure staff develop and implement plans to manage the risk consistent with organizational goals. Monitors progress. Resolves interdepartmental issues related to priorties, budget, time lines, governance, etc.

Responsible: Manages the risk to achieve organizational goals. Makes decisions and esclates issues concering time lines, budgets, priorities, etc.

FIGURE 2.1

Roles and Responsibilities for Common Digital Collection SEO Risk Areas

System Administration	Application Administration	Programmer	Web Design / Developer	Vendor
Accountable	Accountable		Support	Support
Accountable	Support	Accountable		Support
Accountable		Accountable		Support
Responsible				Accountable
Responsible	Support	Support		Support
Accountable	Accountable	Support		Accountable
Support	Responsible	Support	Accountable	Accountable
	Responsible	Accountable	Support	Accountable
Support	Responsible	Support	Support	Accountable
	Responsible	Support	Responsible	Accountable
	Support	Support	Accountable	Accountable
	Support	Support	Accountable	Accountable
	Accountable	Support	Accountable	Accountable
	Accountable	Support	Responsible	Accountable
	Support	Support	Accountable	
	Support		Support	
	Support		Support	Support
	Support		Support	
Support			Support	Accountable
Accountable	Accountable	Support	Accountable	Accountable
	Support	Support		Support

Accountable: Identifies issues, provide options and propose solutions aligned with organizational goals. Ensures solution implemention is working. Accountable to responsible person.

Support: Has skills and ideas to identify and resolve issues.

roles they will need to work with, both upstream and downstream. An example that we'll discuss in detail in chapter 3 is the relationship between sitemaps and robots.txt files. For now we can say that sitemaps are road maps for search engines as they crawl the contents of a repository, and robots.txt files are simple text files that server administrators write to tell crawlers which parts of the web server they may enter, and which are "disallowed." Sitemaps that conflict with robots .txt files only serve to frustrate crawlers and waste their limited time looking for pages you have instructed, intentionally or unintentionally, the search engine not to index. It would seem a simple concept, but this is one of those cases where the administrative/human aspects of SEO trump the technical aspects, and where the all-important issue of communication comes into play. If one person is responsible for sitemaps and another for robots.txt files and those people aren't talking to each other, well, you get the picture. Don't ask why we know this.

Users and crawlers may also be frustrated if digital objects have been moved to another directory or server without a corresponding redirect message that gives a forwarding address. How these redirects are generated depends on the web server software that is installed. Apache web server and Windows IIS have similar functions, but their implementation is different. Systems administrators must be knowledgeable about whatever web server is installed and able to provide an efficient route for the search engine crawler (see chapter 5 for more about redirects).

Applications Administrators

Applications administrators work in the next layer of repository technology, which we refer to as the application layer and is where digital asset management (DAM) software packages are installed. Like systems administrators, applications administrators must recognize barriers to crawlers in this layer. (By the way, sometimes system administrators and applications administrators are the same people). Figure 2.1 contains a number of SEO risks related to the application layer that applications administrators are likely to encounter and the other roles they will need to work with to manage the risks. The barriers thrown up by digital asset management (DAM) systems can include JavaScript, which most search engine

> Most DAM software includes both a database and a presentation layer, and some use relatively simple XML or other flat file databases, but if the database layer relies on a sophisticated relational database (like Oracle, PostgreSQL, MS SQL, or MySQL) you may need a database administrator (DBA) as well as an applications administrator.

crawlers don't like, framesets, multiple URL paths for the same objects, or methods to redirect users that violate search engine policies.

Programmers

Programmers can address a variety of tasks in an automated fashion that would take too long to do manually. For instance, they might develop pattern recognition scripts to match strings of text that are too difficult to find or too numerous to edit by hand. They will also write the code that provides features not provided by your existing application, and that you need to systemically display or alter data. They should know what regular expressions (RegEx) are and have the skills to use RegEx to identify and alter patterns in URLs. They will be familiar with one or more popular web scripting or programming languages like Perl, PHP, JavaScript, C#, or Java. Depending on which database supports your DAM, they may also be required to know how to interact with that database by writing queries in an appropriate language. Programmers are the IT people everyone thinks of when they need a feature or capability that doesn't exist in the off-the-shelf software your organization currently uses.

Website Builders

Web designers and web developers build and manage the website's user experience in the presentation layer. They typically build or modify the splash pages and display templates for digital collections. They play an important role in "on-page" SEO which includes determining how a user navigates the website, how web pages are constructed, what a user sees in his or her web browser, and what search engine crawlers digest. Figure 2.1 contains a number of SEO risks related to the presentation layer that web developers are likely to encounter and the other roles they will need to work with to manage. One potential risk involves the design elements in a website. It's possible for talented designers to create beautiful websites that are completely opaque to search engine crawlers because they consist entirely of graphics or have methods that violate W3C standards. Well-designed websites can provide enticing lead-ins for search engine crawlers by offering text that search engines can index. "High-quality, keyword-rich written content is the single most fundamental element of effective search engine optimization" (Lieb 2009, 42). At the same time, caution must be exercised in the use of keywords in websites to avoid "keyword stuffing," a practice that fills a page with search terms "making it appear very relevant to a search whose query contains one or more of those terms" (Svore et al. 2007).

Even staff who work at the most basic levels of digital library development—scanning documents, for instance—carry responsibility for SEO. Google and other search engines place limits on the size of PDF documents they will index, so those files should be optimized to reduce size while still being readable, and they should also contain searchable text.

Other Important SEO Personnel

Catalogers have provided descriptive information for library collections for ages, and digital collections require the same attention in the form of metadata. Search engine crawlers faced with thousands of digital objects in a given collection want each object to have unique metadata that describes what the digital object is and includes the information your target audience(s) will value (i.e., search for). A particular risk is the cataloger who, faced with thirty photographs of a man on a horse in a given collection, creates the same "Man on horse" title for each. Search engine crawlers that see identical metadata over and over again will give up because they have no way of knowing that each photograph is actually unique, and they think that adding thirty more identical images to their indexes is not bringing value to their customers. In these cases it's probably better to make available online only a sampling of images for which catalogers are able to provide robust descriptions.

New developments in linked data (sometimes known as the semantic web) will open realms of possibility for the way search engines find and relate digital objects to each other. The problem with most current metadata practices is that they fail to establish context and relationships. Let's return to the horse analogy for a moment. The search engine that finds images that refer to "mustang" in their titles has no way of knowing whether the images are of horses or cars, because there's no information that would allow the search engine to understand the context. Linked data attempts to address the problems of context and relationships by using resource description framework (RDF) "triples" that establish a subject-predicate-object relationship. OCLC recently announced that WorldCat now contains the "largest set of bibliographic data on the web," offered up as linked data, and sees growing potential for its use by intelligent crawlers and other commercial applications (OCLC, Inc. 2012). Linked data will help to make information on the Web become much more useful and subject to more accurate retrieval.

Another example of cataloging needs centers on e-science and data management. Metadata for data sets will need to be aligned with all search engines, but in particular with academically oriented search engines like Google Scholar and

Microsoft Academic Search. The role of catalogers is nearly limitless in the digital world, but it requires learning new concepts and frameworks, and a willingness to work in a different paradigm.

Librarians have room for improvement when it comes to promoting the work we do, and effective *marketing and publicity* efforts can help achieve that elusive "link juice" that search engines factor into their indexing and ranking algorithms (Brin and Page 1998; NetLingo 2007). Essentially, the more sites that link to you (particularly reputable, high-quality sites), the more link juice you get. Traditional publicity still works, but the resulting increase in traffic tends to be unsustainable. An effective marketing campaign might include creating a Facebook site or a blog with articles about your repository, or about a particular collection in your repository. As with all things, moderation is the best strategy. Don't create a bunch of sites with links into your repository that you can't maintain, because dead sites don't look too good to a search engine, either. We'll talk more about these strategies in chapter 8.

Software Vendors

This category may seem a bit out of place because *software vendors* are usually external commercial firms that sell their products to libraries. And while it's true that much of our enterprise-level software still comes from those firms, more open source development of software is occurring in libraries, or in developer communities. Regardless of the source of the software, the point we want to make is that software customers have influence with software developers, and the latter should be held accountable for barriers in their software that prevent search engines from accessing or presenting your digital content. Most developers want to improve their products, and if you can demonstrate that a particular DAM or discovery layer has shortcomings that negatively affect your SEO strategies, then those developers will likely be interested in fixing those problems. The alternative is for your staff to fix and maintain the software's shortcoming (assuming the parts of the code you need can be modified) or you live with limited search engine visibility. If the vendor does not think the issue is a priority you may consider an alternative vendor. Just be aware that sophisticated software packages have many moving parts, and that vendors will naturally be cautious about making changes that could have adverse effects elsewhere. Their development schedule may not match your impatience to address immediate problems with donors or administrators. Most every vendor or open source project runs through a natural curve; they tend to be nimble and agile at first and that is an attractive thing. But eventually the software gets sophisticated and the number of clients grows, and nimbleness and agility are lost as the products and the organizations that support them become ponderous and slow to react.

SUMMARY

Our hope for this chapter was to give a high-level managerial overview of search engine optimization. SEO affects many areas of an organization, and in turn there are numerous people who have a stake and play a role in its successful practice. Those roles are best driven from a strategy of alignment with organizational goals, and from the organization's leadership. We'll reiterate once more that SEO is not the domain of the IT department alone; it must be "owned" by the stakeholders who have an interest in the accessibility and visibility of the collections, and in telling the story about how those collections benefit the community.

Chapter Three

How Internet Search Engine Indexing Works

It is hard to define what that "thing" is that you view in a web browser. Is it an object, an item, a page, a document, a book? Some of these terms are legacies from our print world, and don't correspond very well to how information is organized and presented in the digital world, but for simplicity's sake we still use them. A few years ago Google identified over one trillion unique URLs displaying "pages" that could be indexed (Alpert and Hajaj 2008). Incorporating all those pages in a single search engine index is a daunting task, but Google took it on in the late 1990s when it announced its mission: "organize the world's information and make it universally accessible and useful" (Google 1998). As Internet growth exploded over the next decade the task went from daunting to astonishingly complex. In 2010 Comscore reported that Google handled 34,000 queries per second worldwide, or 3 billion per day or 88 billion per month (McGee 2010a). The speed with which search engines like Google are able to respond to all these queries is part of what makes them so popular.

The bombardment of queries with the expectation of instantaneous response makes the job of search engines difficult, but it's actually the easier part of the problem they face because it can be addressed with computing power. The tougher part is the demand that they accurately interpret the intent of searchers with what amounts to very little information. As two presenters put it recently, "imagine a stranger walks up to you and utters two words completely out of context, then stares and waits for a response" (Goodman and Green 2012). In a traditional reference interview there was interaction, a back-and-forth conversation that allowed the librarian to determine context, and to interpret body language and other signals from the user. Search engines have no such luxury. They contend with a paucity of information from users who expect a near miracle of information (and often get it) each time they submit a query. The good search engines perform these miracles with the use of very sophisticated algorithms that weigh over 250 signals that include link structure, keyword analysis, information about the user, and historical data. They need all the help they can get, and that's why it's important to know how search engines work and what they're looking for.

How do search engines determine what to include within their indexes and present in their search engine results pages (SERPs)? Google acknowledges more than 250 factors (Google 2011f) that comprise their "organic search" algorithms, but it's more important to understand that search engine users are customers of the search engines; they are not your customers until they get to your site. Any business needs to take care of its customers by delivering the experiences or the products that the customers are looking for.

> Figure 3.1 illustrates the two main types of search results provided on a SERP: organic and pay-per-click (PPC). This book, and our research, focuses on organic search results.

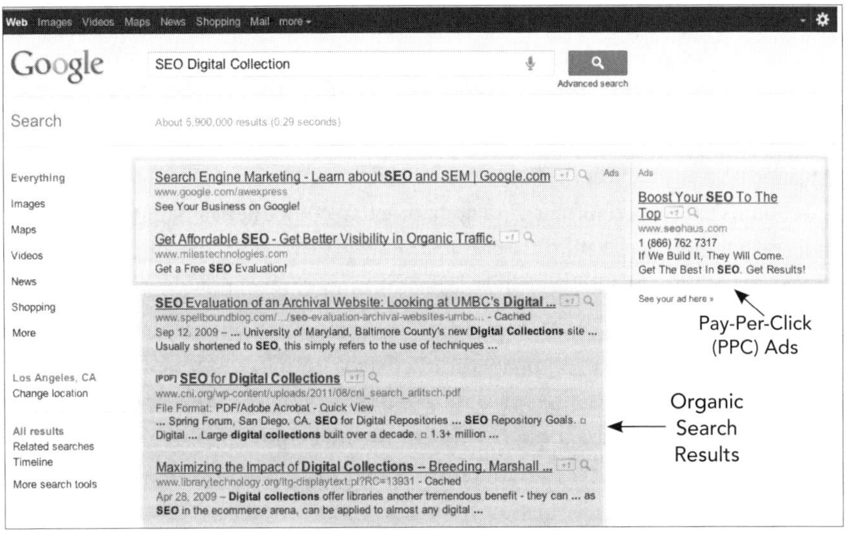

FIGURE 3.1
Search Engine Results Pages (SERP)

How Many Web Pages Exist?

In 2005 Google estimated that in the seven years they had been operational they had indexed less than 1 percent of the world's available information at the time (Schmidt 2005). While the number of unique URLs has increased well past one trillion since then, and the number of websites stands at over 555 million (Alpert and Hajaj 2008; Pingdom 2012), it's estimated that the top three search engines, Google, Bing, and Yahoo!, only contain a maximum of 50 billion pages in their collective indexes as of August 2011 (Kunder 2011).

We like to think of digital repository content as a product, and focus on two simple questions:

> "Is the repository content worthy enough for the search engine's customers?" If the answer is yes, then, like a product retailer, the search engine will want to include that content in its index in case it has a customer that wants access to it. Like a retailer, it only wants to carry products with the potential of delivering an experience that its customers will value.

> "How much will the search engine user value your content?" The answer to this question determines where your product will be displayed on SERPs. The search engine can place your product on the first page of a SERP (the equivalent of eye-level shelf space next to the entrance of a brick-and-mortar retailer) or on page 100 of the SERP (leaving your product in the backroom warehouse).

In this chapter we begin to explain the basics of grabbing the attention of crawler-based search engines such as Google and Bing, and presenting them with content "worthy" of being added to their indexes. It's a complex proposition, and for now we'll stay at a relatively high level, explaining in general terms how search engines acquire information about your content, what they do with it, and what potential barriers they may face. In subsequent chapters we'll provide more detail about factors that affect this process and what you can do to make your content more appealing and your infrastructure more inviting.

HOW SEARCH ENGINES INDEX YOUR CONTENT

When you query a search engine you are not actually searching the Web. Rather, you are searching an index (or indexes) of the content the engine found and chose to include. Modern computing architecture allows indexes to be replicated and distributed throughout the world in massive data centers to handle the load that the world's estimated 2.1 billion Internet users may unleash at any time (Pingdom 2012). Google is secretive about its data centers and locations, but estimates from a few years ago put the number worldwide at thirty-six, nineteen of which are in the United States (Pingdom 2008). That's a lot of data centers for one enterprise, but an even bigger number is the estimated 900,000 servers they house (Miller 2011). Google operates on this massive scale precisely so that it can continue to deliver the best results and to remain at the top of the competitive search engine market.

> Google's lead engineer for search quality, Matt Cutts, published a short but excellent video titled *How Search Works* on YouTube that we highly recommend (Cutts 2010a).

Creating an index in advance is part of what helps a search engine respond so quickly and accurately to queries, but the downside is that it's never quite up-to-date. You will experience this phenomenon most acutely as you wait for a search engine to find and index your content. Search engine indexes are created in three general steps (see figure 3.2).

Crawling

Internet search engines index content by sending "crawlers" (also known as spiders or robots) to websites. The crawlers are seeded with a list of known sites generated from previous crawls and augmented with sitemaps (see "Sitemaps" later in this chapter). The crawler is pointed at a seed site and follows all the links it can find, noting any new sites, changes to existing sites, and links that no longer work (i.e., dead links).

Indexing

The crawler follows links to related pages or objects on the site and "harvests" all the words it sees, noting their location and any tags or attributes used on the

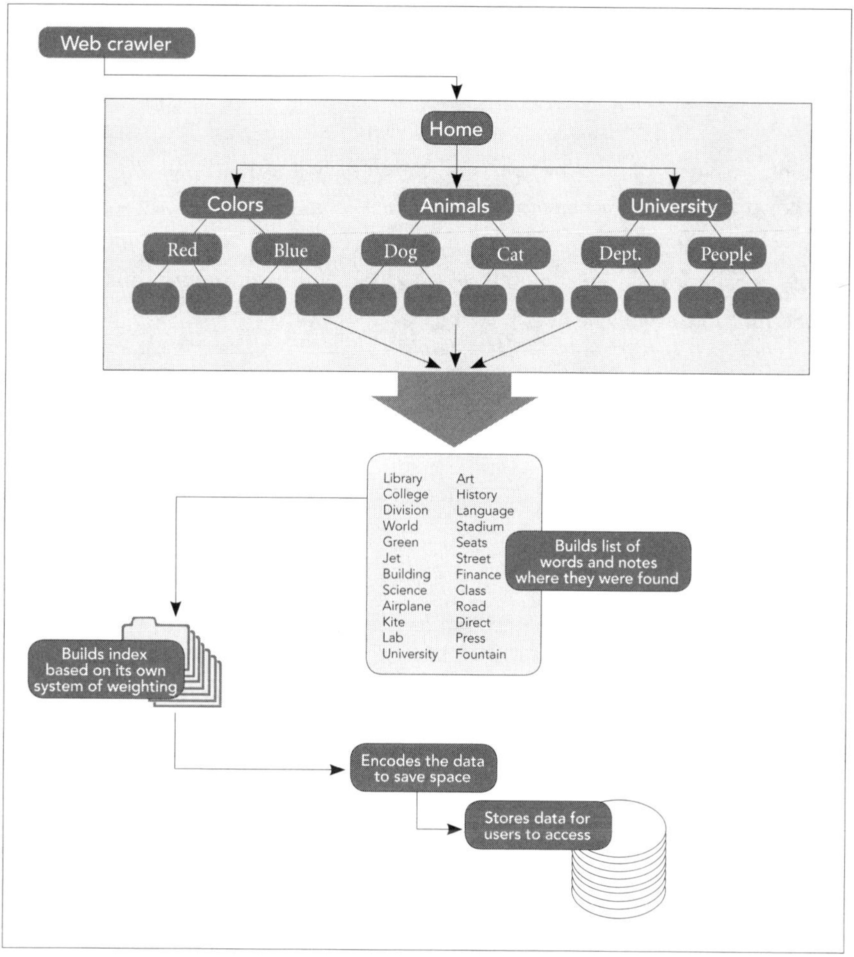

FIGURE 3.2
How Search Engines Work

Speed Matters

New information on the Internet is increasing at a faster rate than search engines can digest it, so your server's response time is incredibly important. Anything that slows the crawler's progress on your site, e.g., spider traps (Wikipedia 2011), server performance, broken links, and so on, equates to a bad experience for search engine users and reduces the chances your content will be admitted to the search engine's index (Singhal and Cutts 2010; Brutlag 2009).

page. The search engine then decides whether the information that's been gathered should be added to its index. It's a simple concept, but there are numerous details and nuances that complicate the process. Server response time, dead links, HTML errors, server and software configurations that create barriers, uniqueness of content, freshness of content, and application of metadata can all affect whether and how thoroughly your site is indexed. Website graphic design features can also throw up barriers to crawlers. Everyone loves an attractive website, but an image-heavy website leaves little to be indexed, and frames and poorly implemented JavaScript can cause navigational problems for crawlers.

Serving Results to the User

Search engines use algorithms that consider many factors in determining what results to return, and the order in which they are presented, in response to a user's search query. One of the primary factors Google made famous was "Page Rank," which is the importance of a page based upon the number and quality of "in-bound" links from other websites (Brin and Page 1998; Page et al. 1998). An in-bound link from another site is like a vote that contributes to your site's page rank, but not all votes on the Internet are equal. For example, a link from a site with very high-quality content and a strong reputation (measured by many in-bound links) like the *New York Times* will add considerably more page rank to your site than a link from the classified section of a small local newspaper or "spammy" link farms.

Search Engine Crawlers Are Blind

As we mentioned in the first chapter, search engine crawlers can be thought of as visually impaired users. Images mean nothing to them unless accompanied by descriptive text. Indexable text is usually the text on the page that is visible in a web browser and that can be spoken by screen reader software, and the placement of a term in a page's construction is almost as important as the fact that it appears at all. In other words, if a term is crucial to describing the content of your site and is a term by which users will search, then it should appear prominently on the page in areas that users and search engines notice (i.e., page title, link anchor text, body text, alt tags, etc.). Always think about helping the user understand the object within your collection and why it's important.

Take heed that Google has incorporated algorithms to "level the playing field" between webmasters who focus on building great websites with quality content and overly aggressive SEO webmasters who produce "webspam" (Cutts 2012; Fox 2012). In early 2012 Google began to warn about a major update to their algorithm they referred to as the "over optimization filter" and then "webspam algorithm," before officially being named "Penguin" (Schwartz 2012c; Schwartz 2012b). The key lesson is to focus on setting systems and processes that address the fundamentals and avoid the mindset that more is better. For example, do not stuff a bunch of keyword-rich links in the page footer using a small font or spend time trying to get the "right" keyword density. These types of efforts do not help the user and search engines are constantly adding filters, and in some cases penalties, so that any benefits you may see are typically short-lived. Search engines change their algorithms faster and more often than most people change their socks, let alone their digital repository websites.

Indexable Text

Providing useful text for search engines to index is a learned skill, and we'll delve much more deeply into the subject in chapter 6. For now we'll just make a few general statements about text:

- How text is written and where it is placed is crucial to getting indexed and to making a good appearance in SERPs.
- Invisible text is generally unacceptable to search engines; they want to "read" what users read.
- Invisible text in the form of meta tags in the <head> section of HTML pages is acceptable, and even encouraged as those tags can be very useful to search engines as machine-understandable text.

What Makes Repositories Different

Objects in a digital repository are contained in a database. Some databases are relational, meaning that the data reside in table structures, and some are flat, meaning tabs, paragraphs, or tags in text-based files provide structure for the data. In either case, web pages that display the objects are generally constructed dynamically, or "on the fly." (See figure 3.3.) A programmed script assembles

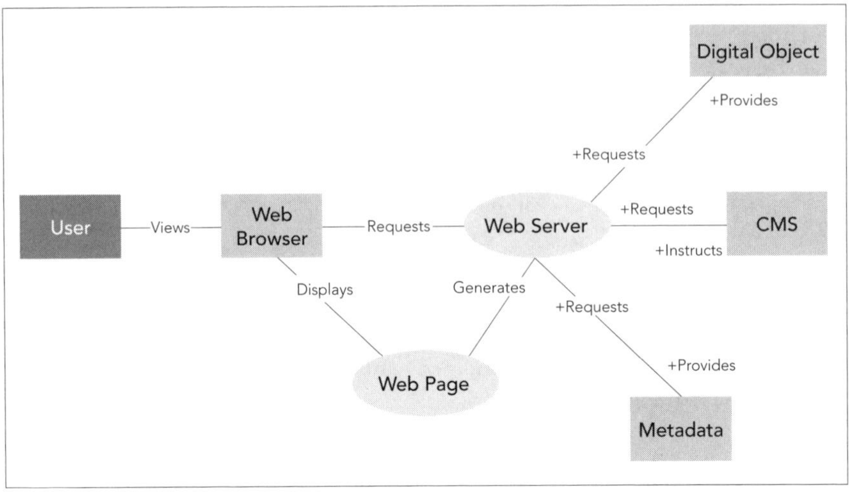

FIGURE 3.3
Dynamic Web Pages

various data components to generate a page at the moment that it is "called" by the user. Calling a page involves clicking on a hyperlink or going directly to a URL to generate its display. Data components may include the object itself (a digitized photograph, for example), the metadata associated with it, and the HTML template that will include a header and footer, along with various other design elements that help make a page useful and attractive.

A search engine crawler does not crawl through a database. It wants to see the compiled page just as the user sees it, so it follows the link for each object in the database and triggers the generation of a page for each. It then harvests the text that is generated for that page before moving on to the next object. It is at this crucial juncture, when the page is displayed, that all the text you hope will be indexed by the search engine must be present, prioritized, and accessible to the crawler.

SITEMAPS

Sometimes search engine crawlers will find your repository because it has been linked from another site. Getting linked from other sites is an SEO strategy that we will discuss in more detail later, but for now let's assume that you have a new site and that you are facing the proverbial chicken and egg problem: getting indexed if no one (including search engines) knows you exist. In these cases the search

```
<?xml version="1.0" encoding="UTF-8"?>
<urlset xmlns:xi="http://www.w3.org/2001/XMLSchema-instance"
    xsi:schemaLocation="http://www.sitemaps.org/schemas/sitemap/0.9 http://www.sitemaps
    .org/schemas/sitemap/0.9/sitemap.xsd" xmlns="http://www.sitemaps.org/schemas/
    sitemap/0.9">
    <url>
        <loc>http://content.lib.utah.edu/<loc>
        <lastmod>2011-08-29</lastmod>
        <changefreq>daily</changefreq>
        <priority>1.0</priority>
    <url>
    <url>
        <loc>http://content.lib.utah.edu/cm4/az.php</loc>     ← Preferred URL
        <lastmod>2011-08-22T1459:53-06-00</lastmod>           ← Last modification date
        <changefreq>daily</changefreq>   ←                      How often content changes
        <priority>0.9</priority>   ←                            Link's relative priority
    <url>
```

FIGURE 3.4
Sitemap

engine may require an invitation to send its crawlers to your site, and this invitation comes in the form of sitemaps.

Sitemaps are XML files that follow a protocol to give search engines a few important pieces of information about your repository: the preferred URLs for its content; when an object was last updated; and how important the object is in relation to the rest of your site. (See figure 3.4.) Sitemaps should contain a URL for every object in your digital repository, which can make them very lengthy files, but the URLs help the crawler quickly find each object in your collection. If generating an XML sitemap sounds difficult, don't worry. Numerous sitemap-generation tools may be found on the Web by searching for "sitemap generator."

Google first introduced sitemaps in 2005, and eventually other search engines announced their support of the sitemaps protocol, which has since been formalized. "Using the Sitemap protocol does not guarantee that web pages are included in search engines, but provides hints for web crawlers to do a better job of crawling your site" (sitemaps.org 2008). Since its original introduction, some search engines have extended the sitemap protocol for specialized files, including video and images, among others.

To aid the process, search engine crawlers like to see an index whose pages are available on the website by checking for a sitemap in the web server's root directory. (In 2011 Google began enforcing its requirement to locate sitemaps in the root directory; sitemaps located in other directories are now ignored.) On larger

> **Google's Webmaster Tools:**
>
> www.google.com/support/webmasters/
>
> **Bing's Webmaster Tools:**
>
> www.bing.com/toolbox/webmaster/

sites, a sitemaps index is also expected in the same root directory. We strongly advise that repository managers ensure these files are free of errors and are kept current and available at all times.

Creating a sitemap alone is not enough. It should also be submitted to the search engine through an established process. Submission processes vary slightly among the major search engines, and instructions for doing so are usually offered on a search engine's Webmaster Support Tools site.

Robots.txt Files

Sometimes there are places on your server where you don't want a crawler to go; you may not want it to crawl through certain directories or to harvest certain objects. A robots.txt file is an accepted exclusion protocol just as a sitemap is an inclusion protocol. It's a simple text file on the server that uses the term "disallow" to discourage crawlers from entering certain directories (see figure 3.5). The robots.txt file is not a security measure and requires the cooperation of the crawler. Malicious crawlers or bots may ignore your request to stay out of certain directories.

It is very important to ensure that your robots.txt file does not conflict with sitemaps you have submitted. In other words, if you invite a search engine crawler into your repository by submitting a sitemap, make sure that it doesn't encounter

```
User-agent: *
Disallow: /cgi-bin/
Disallow: /tmp/
Disallow: /jeff/stuff/junk.html
```

The wild card symbol in the User-agent line indicates that all crawlers are allowed.

FIGURE 3.5
Robots.txt.file

Robots.txt is an efficient tool for communicating instructions to web crawlers on what you do not want crawled on your site using the "Robots Exclusion Protocol." The /robots.txt "standard" is a de facto standard; it is not owned by a standards body or being actively developed (Koster 2010). The systems administrator must know that each search engine has variations and extensions on how they use robots.txt. What works for one search engine does not necessarily work for all search engines. They must also know that robots.txt should not be used to hide or protect information. The file is public and may be used by "spammers" and "hackers" as a road map to exploit website vulnerabilities.

a robots.txt file that "disallows" the very directories that the sitemap has invited it to index. That kind of a conflict wastes crawler time.

SUMMARY

In this chapter we've described the daunting task that search engines have in trying to make sense of the vast amounts of information on the Internet, and to do it in a way that serves their users quickly and accurately. We discussed how search engines find websites and digital repositories, and how they use crawlers to retrieve content to help them create a searchable index. We also talked briefly about the tools that repository managers can use to help facilitate the crawler, and about some common preventable barriers that may stop crawlers from doing their job

In the next chapter we'll describe setting up that all-important feedback loop so that you can understand where your repositories stand with regard to SEO and what needs to be done to improve. We'll get into some very powerful tools—Google Analytics and Webmaster Tools—that will provide tremendously useful information about your users, and about how search engine crawlers fare when they try to index your repositories. It's a crucial chapter because there is some real technique that goes into setting these tools up so they will provide the best information, and in a way that will make the reports accessible and useful to multiple stakeholders in your organization.

Chapter Four

Setting Your SEO Baselines

This chapter will be the most technical thus far, and while the detail may seem overwhelming, at times it's very important for administrators and collection managers to at least grasp the general concepts. Leave the code interpretation and implementation to the IT folks, but know that the decisions you make in implementing the tools we discuss in this chapter will affect your organization's ability to accurately diagnose and address problems, and will affect the kind of reporting you are able to provide to all stakeholders.

In the last chapter we explored the basic characteristics of search engine crawlers, and how they harvest and index content from websites and repositories. We described what crawlers look for in general and explained how to invite them to your repository with sitemaps that provide helpful information about the digital objects within. We also discussed some of the problems that can cause crawlers to stall or fail, and pointed out that many of these problems are the result of misconfigurations of the server and software, or of server performance issues, though crawlers can also be challenged by website design flaws. But how do you know when a crawler is running into trouble? You won't get an e-mail or a phone call. One simple way to tell whether the crawlers are successfully harvesting your site is to search for your digital objects by their titles in a search engine's index, and in fact it was that kind of spot-checking that first helped us realize that something was terribly wrong with our repositories. But it's a method that provides an incomplete picture at best.

You can get a general sense of which of your URLs have been indexed by Google or Bing by performing a search using the "site:" operator, for example, "site:uspace.utah.edu". We say "general" because there are many factors that influence any single SERP. Search engine indexes are in a constant state of flux and are maintained in hundreds of data centers containing hundreds of thousands of servers around the world. Keeping all these servers in sync as content is added and removed is an impossible task (Google 2011d; Autocrat 2009). We also believe that search engines obfuscate certain results to prevent reverse engineering of their proprietary algorithms, and to protect themselves from search engine spam. Thus, the search example shown above will only give you an approximation of what's been indexed, and the result may vary for each search query.

If you've ever built or repaired anything with your hands, you know that the job is far easier and the result much better if you use the proper tools. The same principle applies here; SEO becomes much easier and produces a better result if you use the right tools. Fortunately, search engines like Google and Bing have developed sophisticated (and free) tools that can help you see how well your repository is being indexed, as well as the errors that crawlers produce as they try to harvest your data. Once you see the errors and understand what they mean you will be able to address them. These tools are generally known as "webmaster tools," and we will focus on Google's Webmaster Tools.

A second set of tools will help you gather statistics about visits to your site: how many visitors, where they are from, how often they visit, how long they stay, what operating systems, browsers, mobile devices they use, and so on. Naturally, if you address the errors that crawlers encounter and your indexing ratio goes up, you should see a corresponding increase in visitation. It can go the other way too, though. If you don't address the errors, the crawlers are less productive and may not come back as often, and your indexing ratio will continue to remain low and so will the number of visitors. These tools are generally known as "web analytics" tools or software, and the one we will focus on is called Google Analytics.

In this chapter we will explore both sets of tools in more detail, and will discuss the key issues involved in setting up accounts and profiles in a manner that will ensure long-term and holistic management of all the websites and repositories that are the responsibility of your organization. Setting up these tools correctly will help you manage those sites and gather data about them in a way that provides a seamless picture, rather than constantly having to piece together numbers to create useful reports.

GETTING STARTED

We'll get to the specific tools in a moment, but first we would like to stress a point. It's easy to use the tools provided by Google and Bing. They're free and anyone can establish an account. But it is very important to think of the broader organization you represent, and to consider long-term maintenance and continuity rather than just the few individuals who might currently be responsible for certain aspects of SEO. If a database administrator (DBA) sets up an account using his or her personal Google or Microsoft LiveID account, and begins submitting and managing sitemaps from that account, there will be a serious problem with continuity if he or she then leaves the organization. (We think there's a problem in general with only one person having access to reports.) Likewise, if a systems administrator begins monitoring website visitation from an account separate from the one created by the DBA, there will be partial rather than holistic management. There is a much better way to set up these accounts, and that's our next point of discussion. Communication among staff and coordination of strategy are paramount for successful SEO.

MASTER ACCOUNT VS. PRODUCT ACCOUNTS

The terminology used in Google and Bing accounts can be confusing. Both Google and Bing use a "master account" that gives you access to their "products" (e.g., Webmaster Tools, Analytics, e-mail). (See figure 4.1.) However, the help sections of the individual "products" often also refer to "accounts" within the products. It's crucial to first establish a top-level master account that is associated with your organization and will be used as the administrative account for managing your digital repositories and related websites within the Google or Bing SEO context. The next step is activating the "products" (e.g., Webmaster Tools, Analytics) that are often referred to as "accounts" in the support documentation.

We recommend that accounts be established in the following manner:

Create a mailing list (listserv) on your institution's list server, calling it something like "seo@institution.edu," and subscribe a few key people, such as IT managers, collection managers, and administrators.

Create the organization's master account in Google Accounts or Microsoft Windows LiveID using the address established for the mailing list described above.

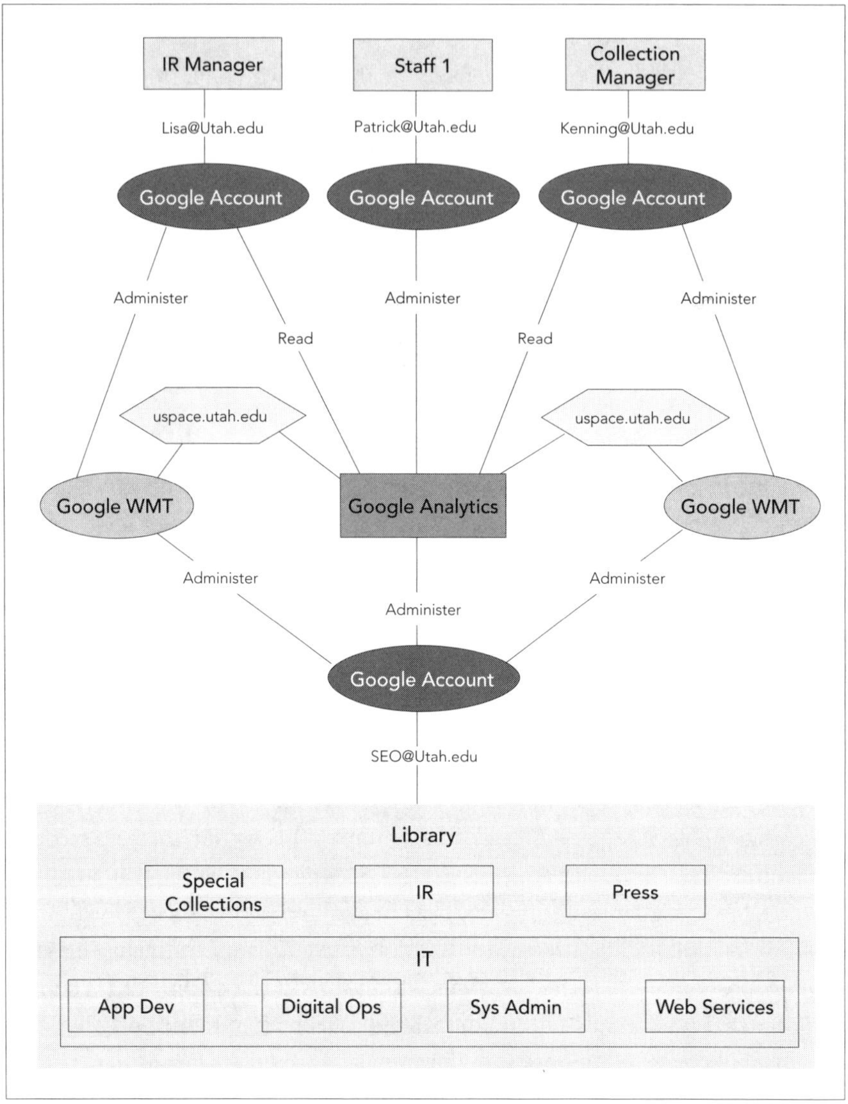

FIGURE 4.1
Google Master Account

Allowing staff to use anything other than an institutional e-mail as their Google Account or MS Live ID primary e-mail address will make long-term administration difficult. This is due to the often creative, esoteric, and inconsistent naming conventions individuals dream up, and it is further compounded by the fact that you will have no way to look up the individual's organizational information (i.e., name, department, supervisor, phone number, and so on) when he uses an e-mail address like jellybean627@gmail.com as opposed to firstname.lastname@institution.edu (or whatever convention is standard at your institution).

Ask individuals who are to have access to the products to establish their own Google Accounts or Microsoft Windows LiveID, using their organization's e-mail address (e.g., firstname.lastname@institution.edu)

Administer individual user access to your institution's "products" using the account established by the individual in step #3. This will ensure that the individuals have access only to the products that are relevant to their roles and responsibilities within your organization.

BE THE MASTER OF YOUR DOMAIN

The next step is defining the physical and logical domains of your digital repositories and their supporting websites. Setup is easy if all your content is stored on a single web server. However, most organizations have multiple servers, with content spanning several domains, subdomains, and subdirectories. If users visit your website and click on a link that takes them into a repository on a different domain or subdomain you have to be able to track them, otherwise your statistics become incomplete and lose considerable meaning. You will miss the indicators that show how visitors arrived at your website, and whether they achieved any of the goals established for your digital repository (e.g., downloads, submissions, purchases, and so on).

Define Your Logical Domain

The logical domain consists of the people inside the organization who have final say about how the content of a given collection or repository is represented and managed. These are usually higher-level administrators whose departments have acquired or created a collection or repository. Photographs, manuscripts, or rare books collections are usually the domain of a special collections director; the institutional repository may fall under a scholarly communication or collections director; and the academic press director will manage a university press collection. Logical domains may vary from one organization to another, but these stakeholders will be keenly interested in how the digital versions of their collections fare in terms of visitation and downloads, and they will benefit tremendously from rising statistics that they can report to their constituents, including donors, funding agencies, staff, and next-level administrators. Providing the stakeholders with useful numbers, regardless of which way they are trending, will win strong advocates when action is needed from staff in their departments.

Inventory Your Physical Domain

The physical domain represents the servers, domains, subdomains, and URLs that comprise the digital library. You will be able to create meaningful reports if you know who's responsible for various websites and the domain/subdomain combinations they cross. You need to know who administers the various host names, which include the domains, subdomains, and subdirectories containing your content. Some of this administration will occur within the library or archives, while other domains may be administered elsewhere on campus or beyond. The best way to keep track of it all and to configure things properly is to create an inventory that relates to your organizational structure. This will help you understand what you control and what you don't. The sites that you control will allow you to alter pages or include code. Sites that are out of your control don't allow you that ability, but good communication with the owners may go a long way toward getting what you need. Website entry points and exit points matter, because they help define your users, what they are doing, how they got there, and where they went. This scenario is magnified in a distributed digital library situation, where your institution may manage a server that aggregates metadata, but where the actual digital objects reside in repositories at other institutions.

Domain names are at the highest point in the hierarchy (e.g., utah.edu, digital newspapers.org, or uofupress.com). The next level in the hierarchy is *subdomains*. Subdomains are typically used to define a physical concept, like a department, function, service, or topic with a relative dependency on the larger domain. For example, the University of Utah's Institutional Repository is managed by the library and can be found at uspace.utah.edu. In this case the library does not control the larger domain "utah.edu" but does control the subdomain "uspace.utah .edu." *Subdirectories*, or folders, are the last level and are typically used to organize files within a domain or subdomain. For example, the URL "uspace.utah.edu/ economics/" indicates "utah.edu" is the domain name, "uspace" is a subdomain, and "economics" is a subdirectory.

The "www" typically preceding a domain name is not actually considered part of the domain, and is in fact, a subdomain. Whenever moving content to a new URL, we prefer to not include the "www" in the URL, because it unnecessarily lengthens and complicates the URL, making it a bit harder to communicate orally and to remember. It's so much easier to speak the words "uspace-dot-utah-dot-edu" than "double-u, double-u, double-u-dot-uspace-dot-utah-dot-edu." The marketing part of SEO includes the ability to easily communicate your message, and your site name is a big part of the message. Just be sure that your web server administrator has configured the website to display without the "www."

WEBMASTER TOOLS

Webmaster Tools are offered both by Google and Bing to assist your technical team in identifying and addressing issues that will help your site perform better in search results. The search engine's crawlers report information about each site you have verified via the Webmaster Tools product (see sidebar). In the next chapter we will discuss specific error messages and how to address them, but for now we'll just list the general ways in which Webmaster Tools can help to get your baseline data stream started:

Google, and most major search engines, use a technique to prevent "host crowding" when serving SERPs, which means that Google will show up to two results from each host name/subdomain of a domain name (Cutts 2007). This ensures no single website will dominate a SERP. If you have a large number of collections that cover similar topics in your repository, then it's advisable to organize your collections around subdomains that define the collection or topic area (e.g., economics.uspace.utah.edu) rather than subdirectories (e.g., uspace.utah.edu/economics/). This will increase the chance that two items from each collection are presented in the SERPs instead of just two items from your entire digital repository.

- Identify which parts of your site pose problems for crawlers.
- Notify the search engine of new or revised XML sitemaps.
- Generate and analyze your robots.txt files.
- Remove URLs from the crawl when they no longer exist (not the same as moving content).
- Identify issues with your page titles and meta tags.
- Identify the top search terms used to reach your site.
- Review pages as the search engine crawler would see them.
- Provide notifications of any quality guideline violations.

Google Webmaster Tools will allow you to add a site using any combination of domain, subdomain, and/or subdirectory, but will not give you access to information until you "verify ownership," which is accomplished by demonstrating the ability to upload a file to the site you have defined (Google 2011a).

GOOGLE ANALYTICS

Once you have improved the crawling and indexing of your site, you will want to review data that can help achieve more visibility with your target audiences. Numerous commercial and free website analysis software tools are available. Some of them analyze web server logs, while others, like Google Analytics, utilize page-tagging techniques that embed code into each page of a website to set and track "cookies." With page tagging, the code sends a message each time a page is viewed. Those data are usually gathered by a third-party system that resides elsewhere and determines visitor information concerning sessions, page views and traffic sources (i.e., referring sites, search terms, and so on). There are advantages and disadvantages to both methods, and we suggest using Google Analytics (which utilizes page tagging) for its ease of use, zero cost, excellent support, and power. If configured properly, Google Analytics can provide information about your logical domain that will help you understand where visitors are coming from and what they are looking for. Aside from creating a Google Account, configuring the Google Analytics product, and embedding a bit of code in each web page HTML header, there is no further overhead for basic reporting. The code is easily embedded in a batch action in sites that employ a content management or template-based system, as is the case with most sizable modern websites or repositories. In addition to using Google Analytics, you should also ensure your web server logs are properly configured for collecting useful information (see sidebar).

Google Analytics provides powerful (but anonymous) data about visitors to your site, their behavior while they're visiting, and the tools they use to view your site. It can also help you to quickly troubleshoot problems on your site. For instance, you may learn that some users have bookmarked and are still visiting an obsolete page that's never been deleted from your server, or that certain page titles are inaccurate or could be written more descriptively. The Google Analytics product can provide the following pieces of information, among others, about your site and its visitors:

- How many unique and returning visitors view your site
- Which search terms they used to reach a page on your website
- What operating system and browser they use
- Whether they use a mobile device to visit your site and which one
- What site pages they landed on and exited from
- What pages they viewed most, the order in which they viewed them, and for how long
- Which countries and cities they are in
- How long your pages take to load

Google Analytics even allows you to establish and track goals. For example, you might want to see which academic papers were downloaded from your institutional repository, and if Google Analytics is set up properly, you may view the results

While we advocate using Google Analytics, analyzing server log files is the way to perform hard-core SEO. If you decide to bring in an SEO consultant or want more detail than Google Analytics provides, you must configure your web server log files to use the W3C's Extend Log File Format for IIS web servers, and Apache Custom Log Format for web servers running Apache. This is a fairly easy setting for your web server administrator to make. Because these formats collect additional data (i.e., bytes delivered, time taken, cached hits, and so on), the logs can also prove very useful in making more informed decisions about optimizing your physical web servers' environment, such as server load balancing and bandwidth needs. It's also important that you make sure your web server administrator regularly closes out the log file and starts a new one to keep log file sizes manageable. This housekeeping is typically done on a daily basis and can be automated.

by college, department, and author. This can help you inform faculty about the frequency with which their papers are accessed, and perhaps will help generate support for increased faculty institutional repository (IR) participation.

There are numerous other data points that Google Analytics provides. A new feature called "In-page Intelligence" shows the links visitors click most on your home page, mimicking some aspects of usability testing. Most of the data can be exported, allowing you to further manipulate the statistics and work them into presentations or reports.

The information that Google Analytics provides creates a feedback loop that can help repository managers improve the user experience and identify what is working well and what is not. It can help improve the text describing a given page, resulting in a better fit with the traffic sources and search queries that deliver users to your site.

CONFIGURING YOUR BASELINE SEO PRODUCTS

While it makes sense to have described Webmaster Tools and Google Analytics in that order, it's actually easier to set them up in the opposite order. Setting up the Google Analytics product first will allow you to begin collecting baseline data, and will streamline the Google Webmaster Tools website verification process.

The Google Analytics Product

Activate the Google Analytics product from the Google Account you've set up with the organizational mailing list (e.g., seo@university.edu). The interface changes occasionally, but the basic steps require you to:

- Go to the Google Webmaster Tools site at http://google.com/webmasters/tools/
- Add a site URL
- Verify the site
- Select Google Analytics from the "Alternate Methods" tab.

Key Concepts

Google Analytics makes it very easy to report on a single physical domain or subdomain. However, if you are like most digital repository managers you have your logical domain (e.g., Special Collections, IR, University Press) spread across multiple physical domains and subdomains. If so, we advise using cross-domain tracking to share or pass information about visitors' activity. To optimize your configuration, you should understand the meaning of Google Analytics' basic terminology: account, web property, profile, and site.

Account is an administrative concept and refers to the organization's master account (e.g., seo@institution.edu). An account has one or more web properties. A *web property* is defined by a domain, subdomain, or subdirectory combination, and includes one or more profiles. The *profile* is used to define which data are collected from the web property's click-stream. The Google Analytics account, web property ID, and profile define the reporting an end user can access.

When you activate the product, Google Analytics creates a "Google Analytics Account" and assigns a unique code to identify both the account and the web property. The account code typically looks like this: UA-12345678-1. The first set of numbers up to the first hyphen is the unique account code, and the "1" following the second hyphen indicates the web property defined within the account. Any web page containing the code (e.g., UA-12345678) is considered part of the Google Analytics Account. The combination of the account and web property ID is referred to as a "site" for reporting in Google Analytics. The Google Analytics administrator is mostly concerned with (1) configuring the web property ID and ensuring all the web pages within his logical domain contain the appropriate Google Analytics code; and (2) using physical domain information to define profiles that represent the logical domain that stakeholders (e.g., IR, Special Collections, University Press) can view.

Cross-Domain Tracking

While there are many configuration options for Google Analytics, we advise configuring a single web property so that it contains the domain of the digital repository that is under your control. You can then use profiles to capture click-stream data relevant to the logical domains you support.

The following physical domains represent some of the digital library at the University of Utah:

- lib.utah.edu
- content.lib.utah.edu
- uspace.utah.edu
- uofupress.com

Cross-domain tracking helps track users when they are referred from one physical domain to another. For many digital repositories, the information describing a collection is contained in one physical domain (e.g., a website located at uspace.utah.edu), while the actual objects in the collection are located within a different physical domain (e.g., a repository located at content.lib.utah.edu). Without cross-domain tracking set up, all you will know is that visitors were referred from one physical domain to the other. The critical information about the links and search terms used that led to viewing or downloading the object within the digital repository (content.lib.utah.edu) will not be passed from the visitors' entry point (uspace.utah.edu).

In other words, you won't know why visitors were referred to your repository, or how they got there. Cooperation among domains will allow you to identify and influence key elements concerning the visibility of your content within SERPs. Some of the items we will discuss in chapter 6 of the book include in-bound linking, keyword phrasing, and synonyms.

The key element in the Google Analytics code you must get right is the _setDomainName command used to set the document.domain cookie variable in the visitors' browser when they visit your websites. Most of the University of Utah's digital repository objects are contained at content.lib.utah.edu. As mentioned earlier, the library does not control the primary domain utah.edu and we are interested in cross-domain tracking of subdomains within our control. This requires us to add the following Google Analytics code to the three primary physical domains. All pages containing lib.utah.edu, including content.lib.utah.edu, would have the following customization in the <head> section of the HTML code.

```
_gaq.push(['_setDomainName', '.lib.utah.edu']);
```

It is important to include the period (.) before the lib.utah.edu. This tells Google Analytics to share information between all subdomains containing "lib.utah.edu." Without the leading period in front of lib.utah.edu, Google Analytics would treat visitors to lib.utah.edu that are then passed to content.lib.utah.edu as separate visits and only log the transfer as a referral. You are not required to make any adjustments to links or forms cross-linking between these subdomains.

Below are the customizations for two physical domains that are within the University of Utah digital repository logical domain:

uofupress.com would include _gaq.push(['_setDomainName', 'uofupress.com']);

uspace.utah.edu would include _gaq.push(['_setDomainName', 'uspace.utah.edu']);

You will also need to add a small customization to each cross-link between sites. For example, any page linking to the home page at uspace.utah.edu from the physical domain lib.utah.edu, or content.lib.utah.edu, would use the code below.

```
<a href="http://uspace.utah.edu/" onclick="_gaq.push(['_link',
'http://uspace.utah.edu/']); return false;">USpace</a>
```

Are there terms that are searched more often than others and can you incorporate more in-bound links in your sites? If your library or archive is part of a consortium you may have a better chance of influencing the other domains in the relationship. You may ask other libraries to link to certain pages or provide certain terminology, but unless you have set up cross-domain tracking in Google Analytics, you will only know that another library is referring visitors to your site, but have no insight into how they got there or what they did that led them to your digital repository.

Measuring Site Performance

Site performance is another important variable that can affect both crawlers and visibility within SERPs, and thus, visitors to your site. A few slow pages can degrade the average speed of your site. Crawlers may give up if your site's pages load too slowly (they've got other sites to harvest), and Google has indicated that it considers site performance in its algorithms and is less inclined to send its users your way if they will suffer delays (Singhal and Cutts 2010). Google Analytics allows you to identify the pages that are loading slowly; they will be revealed in the Page Load category in the Google Analytics dashboard. Causes of slowness may be server-related, but could also be poorly written scripts or complicated designs that call numerous other files from remote sites to compile the page.

Page Load information in Google Analytics can also reveal pages that may be obsolete or orphaned, but that users are somehow still finding. Knowing that those pages are still being found will help you to remove them from the search engine indexes and provide redirects to newer or more appropriate pages.

See box on page 50 for more helpful codes to use with Google Analytics.

Profiles and Filters

The account you establish with Google Analytics will gather raw data from all the domains and subdomains in your jurisdiction. A *profile* allows you to permanently

Include the _trackPageview command to your Google Analytics code. Below is an example from the home page of the University of Utah's Marriott Library:

```
<script type="text/javascript">

var _gaq = _gaq || [];
_gaq.push(['_setAccount', 'UA-12345678-1']);
_gaq.push(['_setDomainName', '.lib.utah.edu']);
_gaq.push(['_setAllowLinker', true]);
_gaq.push(['_trackPageview']);

(function() {
var ga = document.createElement('script'); ga.type = 'text/javascript';
ga.async = true; ga.src = ('https:' == document.location.protocol ?
'https://ssl' : 'http://www') + '.google-analytics.com/ga.js';
var s = document.getElementsByTagName('script')[0]; s.parentNode.
insertBefore(ga, s);
})();

</script>
```


exclude information, whereas a *filter* allows you to temporarily include and exclude. You can give an individual access to a profile. The steps are:

- Create a master profile without any filters or alteration (raw feed). This creates an unadulterated data set, from which you can generate post-filtered profiles.
- Create a second profile that appends cross-domain information (if doing cross-domain data gathering; for details see https://developers.google.com/analytics/devguides/collection/gajs/gaTrackingSite#keyComponents).
- Apply a filter to exclude staff IP addresses (staff visits to websites can skew results, particularly if they are working on the sites).
- Create sub-profiles to give access to specific individuals based on their interests.

Event Tracking

Event Tracking is a Google Analytics feature that allows you to monitor specific user interactions with your website, particularly those that are non-HTML based. For instance, as we've mentioned previously, IR managers would find it very useful to monitor how often users download particular PDF documents. Other collection managers might want to track user interactions with embedded videos or sound files, and others might want to see whether users click more on one type of graphic than another. The possibilities for gathering statistics with Event Tracking are numerous (Google 2012c).

We've hinted already that Google Scholar operates a little differently than Google, and Event Tracking in Google Analytics reveals one of those differences. When Google Scholar indexes PDF documents from institutional repositories, it bypasses any HTML code that is associated with those documents and links directly to the PDF files. It's good for users since it gets them to the document they're looking for more quickly, but it also means a loss of context because the HTML repository page that shows the metadata for the document is bypassed. More important (for statistics-gathering purposes) it means that no call is made to Google Analytics because the code resides in the HTML <head> section that has been bypassed. And if no call is made, then those PDF downloads from your IR are not counted in the stats that Google Analytics provides.

As always, there is a solution. A PHP wrapper can be applied to any request for non-HTML files (i.e., PDF, audio, video); the wrapper uses a mod-rewrite which captures that event and sends the info to your Google Analytics profile (Jackson 2010).

Setting Up Webmaster Tools

Most of the configuration work and SEO optimization takes place in Google Analytics, which is why we had you set that up, first. But Google Analytics won't get any data if your sites aren't getting indexed, and Webmaster Tools is where you ensure that indexing is occurring. To set it up, go to the Webmaster Tools website and log in with your organization's Google Account (e.g., seo@institution.edu). Then click "Verify" to verify ownership of the Google Analytics account. This is the beginning of the feedback loop. (See figure 4.2.)

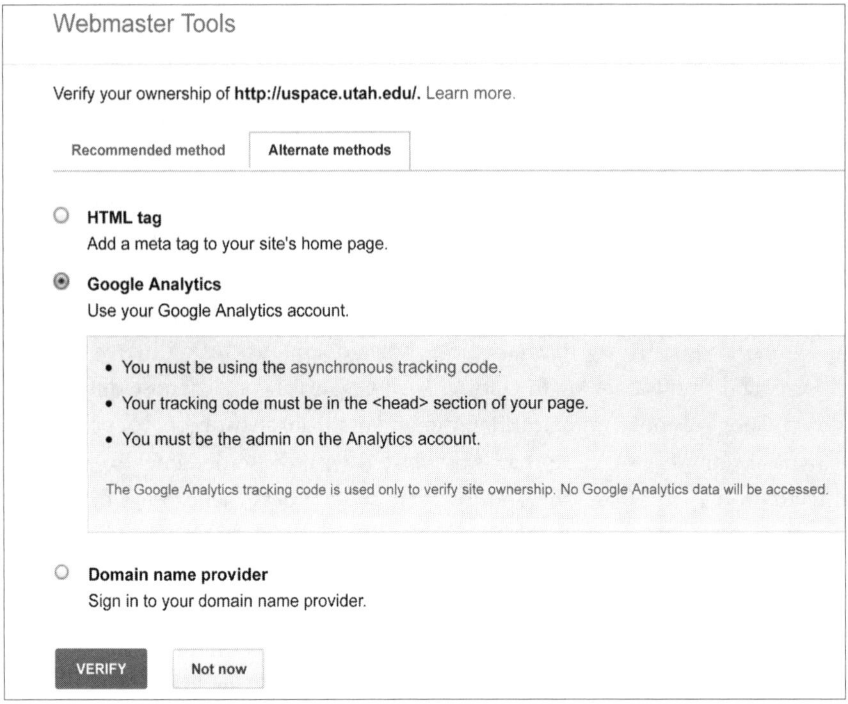

FIGURE 4.2
Webmaster Tools Verify via Google Analytics

When you add new sites to Webmaster tools you also have to assign their owners. Once again, use the institutional mailing list (e.g. seo@institution .edu) to log in to Webmaster Tools. "Claim" the physical websites from which you've inserted the Google Analytics code on the home page. Then add the appropriate staff member as an owner, using their @institution.edu e-mail address (Google 2011c).

SUMMARY

Now that you have set up Google Analytics and Webmaster Tools you will be able to gather data about your visitors and correct errors reported by crawlers. The detail in this chapter may have been difficult to comprehend at times, but the concepts and tools we described are vital to the SEO process. Improving your search engine-indexing ratio is only half the battle; you also have to be able to monitor this dynamic environment and make adjustments when necessary, and you have to be able to produce good data to show the results of your work. Webmaster Tools and Google Analytics are designed to help drive more traffic to your repositories, and learning how to use these sophisticated products is well worth the effort.

In the next chapter we'll define search engine-indexing ratio, and we'll start putting Webmaster Tools to work. We'll examine specific crawler errors revealed by Webmaster Tools and show you how to begin eliminating them. We'll also discuss optimizing site structure and navigation, simplifying URLs, and providing appropriate messages for crawlers if you have to move files, directories, or even domains. As usual, communication among staff plays a huge role in how well your organization can address these issues.

Chapter Five

What Is Your Search Engine-Indexing Ratio and How Can You Improve It?

We've mentioned *search engine-indexing ratio* in preceding chapters, so this is a good time to pause and define the phrase. It's simple. Search engine-indexing ratio is the number of URLs from your repository that are included in a search engine's index divided by the number of URLs you have submitted to the search engine through a sitemap. Obviously you want that ratio to be as high as possible, though it is unlikely that you will reach 100 percent for your entire repository. The ratio is not static. It can change from one crawl to the next, and it is this fluctuation that makes it so important to think of SEO as a dynamic process that must be continually monitored to achieve success. Members of an SEO team must react if a repository's indexing ratio declines dramatically, as there will almost certainly be corresponding crawler error messages that can be investigated and addressed through the tools we introduced in chapter 4. While Google does not have a hard crawl budget that predetermines the number of pages they are willing to crawl on your site, there is a limit to the time and resources they are willing to commit to crawling your website (Enge 2010). A search engine crawler cannot waste its limited resources on your site waiting for pages to load, trying to crawl pages that have errors, are inaccessible to the public, or represent duplicate content. New errors are usually introduced when changes are made to a repository or the server on which it resides, and those errors can cause indexing ratios to decrease, or, in extreme cases, cause crawlers to drop your repository from the search engine's index altogether.

In this chapter we'll delve more deeply into optimizing your web server for crawlers by minimizing the number of errors they generate while trying to harvest your content. We won't get into very much technical detail because our goal is to help you understand the concepts rather than the exact steps needed to address them. We'll identify the most common errors and discuss etiquette, which is practiced by leaving appropriate messages if you move your repository content or make other changes. We'll introduce server-based redirection techniques to get users to the content they want, even if they've entered an incorrect URL. And we'll talk about optimizing site structure and site speed to improve the user experience. The number of crawler errors can seem frightening at first; Webmaster Tools reported more than 100,000 errors per crawl in our environment before we began practicing good SEO techniques. But the errors are not so intimidating when you recognize what they mean and how you can address them in batches.

IDENTIFYING AND ELIMINATING CRAWLER ERRORS

Crawlers report a variety of errors through the Webmaster Tools offered by Google and Bing. The table below shows some of the most common errors and general solutions for addressing them.

Oops! Custom Error Pages

Search engine crawlers are the biggest concern when trying to address errors that affect your indexing ratio, but you also don't want to frustrate your users, especially if those users operate their own websites and might link to your site from theirs. The "link juice" these other sites provide is enormously important because search engines take notice of your site's popularity, and it affects your indexing ratio as well as ranking. The people in the organization who must address errors tend to be a combination of systems administrators and programmers, but someone else may be in charge of monitoring the errors through Webmaster Tools.

Your web server's default error messages are not informative and are very unattractive (see figure 5.1). This creates a disconcerting experience for users who have mistyped a URL or clicked on a link no longer connected to an active page.

The blow can be softened a bit by serving up a page that looks familiar and carries a message that is both apologetic and helpful (see figure 5.2).

In this customized 404 Error page the user sees a branded message that offers options for finding the page they are looking for, including an e-mail help address

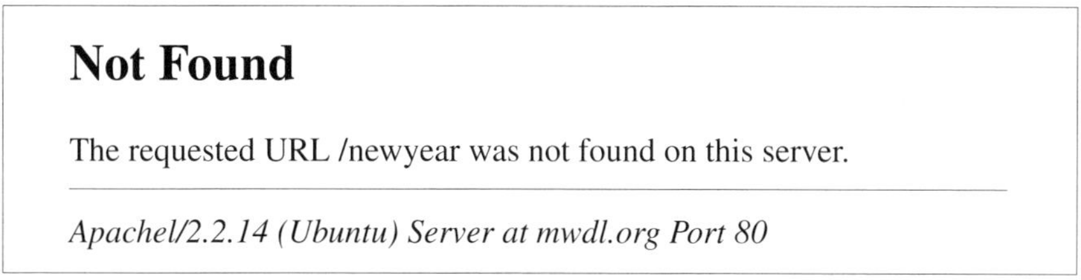

FIGURE 5.1
Default "Page Not Found" (404) Error Message

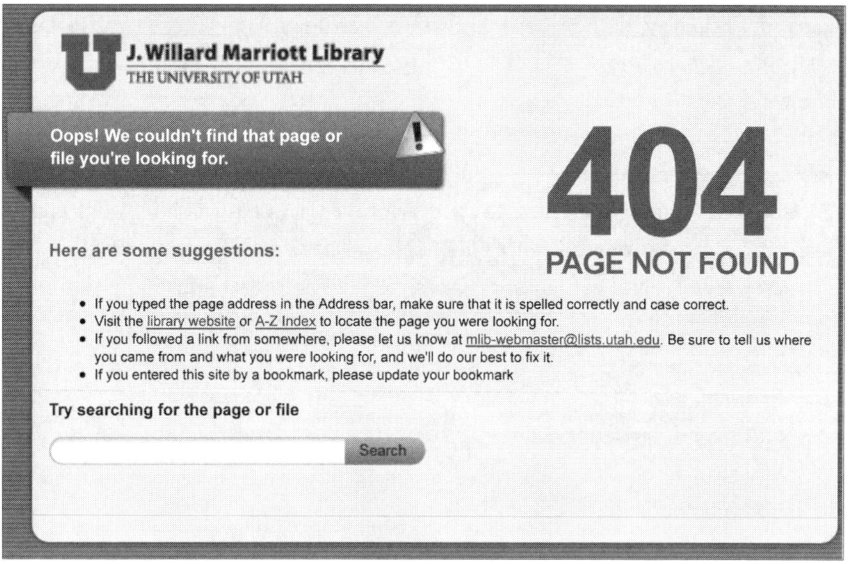

FIGURE 5.2
Customized "Page Not Found" (404) Error Message

and a search box that allows the user to try to locate the missing page on your site. Usually a web designer creates this attractive and informative customized page, and a systems administrator configures the server to call it when the expected page is not found.

The other custom error pages that should be created and configured on your web server are:

Gone (HTTP 410)—"The page you requested no longer exists and there is no forwarding address"

Forbidden (HTTP 403)—"The page you requested is protected and requires you to log in"

Temporarily Unavailable (HTTP 503)—"The page you requested is temporarily unavailable. Please check back in [60 minutes, 3 weeks, etc.]" [Ensure the system admin sets the time to check back in the HTTP header for the benefit of crawlers]

It is very difficult to eliminate all crawl errors from a large, dynamic website. HTTP 404 and robots.txt errors are to be expected (Google 2012b; Moskwa 2011). However, many unintentional mistakes that are made by web teams can trip up crawlers and users, and search engine tools now provide feedback to help web teams check their work. For example, if you are getting robots.txt errors you should make sure they are for the specific directories and pages you do not want crawled; we have seen cases where the robots.txt file prevented Google from crawling *any* of the repository's content. The SEO team should confirm the 404 and robots.txt errors being reported are the ones they expected.

Webmaster Tools will list several other error messages returned by crawlers that have experienced problems with your repositories. The following errors always waste crawler time and can, in some cases, negatively impact your SERP rankings:

1. Soft 404s
2. In sitemaps
3. URLs not followed
4. URLs timed out
5. URL unreachable

It is best to address as many of these crawl errors as possible.

Google has stated that it "currently" treats 410 errors the same as 404 errors (Moskwa 2011). However, that can change, and in our experience nonconformity with a recommended standard or practice can negatively affect index ratio, SERP ranking, or both, at a later date and without warning. We once had our sitemaps stored in a server subdirectory, despite Google's request that they be at the server root. It was okay until Google suddenly decided to enforce its request in August 2010, and our indexing ratio fell precipitously. We moved the sitemaps to the root and the ratio began to increase again.

Error Code	Description	Solution
403	Web server error that indicates the restricted nature of a page. It usually requires a log-in, but the crawler doesn't know the log-in information, so it's wasting its time trying to get in.	Include "no follow" text in HTML links to the page and "no index" in the page's HTML header (Google 2011e).
404	Web server error that indicates the file can't be found. The page doesn't exist at that URL.	Configure web server to respond with HTTP 404 error code and serve a custom 404 page that informs the user and offers helpful suggestions (Google 2011b).
Soft 404	Search engines don't like when they request a specific page and your server responds with an HTTP 200, i.e., "everything is good and we are working on serving up the page you requested" and then your server redirects them to a different page. This type of activity is confusing for users, and is sometimes used by "black hat" SEO practitioners to mislead users. Moreover, it wastes crawlers' time looking for pages that don't exist.	If the page never existed, configure the web server to respond with an HTTP 404. If the page has been removed, the web server should respond with an HTTP 410 error. In both cases serve a custom 404 page to inform the user and offer helpful suggestions.
503	Planned maintenance, server errors, under construction pages, etc.	Configure the web server to return an HTTP 503 error to indicate the error is temporary, include a time estimate for when the site/page will be up again, and serve a custom 503 page to inform users about the temporary nature of the problem and ask them to check back later (Honen and Szymanski 2011).

SORRY, WE'VE MOVED (REDIRECTS)

Moving is a fact of life, even in the digital world. Occasionally it becomes necessary to move files, directories, and even servers. Just as in our physical lives, it's important in the digital world to leave forwarding addresses. These are known as redirects, and they quickly reroute crawlers and users to the new locations. Redirects address the etiquette we referred to in the introduction (users and crawlers alike appreciate politeness). Failure to provide redirects can cause both users and crawlers to arrive at dead ends, because they have addresses (URLs) for items they've been told are there. Without redirects those dead URLs will leave both users and crawlers frustrated.

Of course, the situation in the digital world tends to be a bit more complicated than the physical world. If you move from Wisconsin to Utah you only have one address to change. But moving from one content management system to another can leave hundreds of thousands of item URLs stranded if you don't have a systematic way of redirecting users and crawlers to the new addresses. The table, below, shows two of the most common HTTP redirect codes.

Code	Description	Use
301	Permanent redirect	Use when the site or objects have moved to a new, permanent location and the URL is not going to change.
302	Temporary redirect	Use when the new URL is not yet stable. Search engines won't purge you from their index but won't list every page in search results until the new location becomes permanent.

A 301 redirect is a trustworthy way to inform search engines that you have moved. Most of the trust you have built up for the page, subdirectory, or domain travels to the new home. Without the redirect you lose link juice and your site is treated as a brand-new member of the web community; it takes time to rebuild the trust.

Redirects must be used with care, since they have occasionally been used with malicious intent to fool search engines. As with other aspects of SEO, it usually takes a team to address redirects. Someone must create a lookup table to map the old URLs to the new, and then someone else, usually a programmer, must create a pattern recognition script using regular expressions (i.e., RegEx) to match strings of text. A server administrator then configures the server to implement the developed processes in real time.

A web server's normal response to a request is to immediately issue a standard HTTP 200 ("everything's okay") response when it serves the requested page. Use 301, 404, 410 or other JavaScript responses prior to issuing an HTTP 200 response, never afterward. Issuing the response afterward is a "black hat" SEO technique and creates trust issues with search engines. Unless you are sure the switch will help the user (e.g., a word in your URL is often misspelled by users), search engines will penalize your content or ban your site altogether. Search engines have gone as far as recommending that websites serve a custom 404 error page that helps the user understand their request received a 404 (page not found) and waiting a full 10 seconds before redirecting the user to your home page (Ohye 2008).

Canonical Links

Digital objects in a database often have more than one URL. When search engines determine that the same, or similar, object has multiple URLs, they will typically apply a SERP ranking penalty for duplicate content, because duplication is an old "black hat" SEO technique used to SPAM the search engine index. Creating canonical links is an acceptable "white hat" SEO tool to specify your preferred URL for the requested page (Google 2011g).

Mod_Rewrite and Mod_Redirect

Mod_rewrites and mod_redirects are useful web server functions that are very powerful SEO tools. They can help make the visitation experience easier for users and crawlers by moving the burden of redirection to an automated internal web server function that is executed independently of the web application, often eliminating the need for customizing your web application code for changes to your content's location (i.e., URL).

Basically, the mod_rewrite and mod_redirect functions are used to alter the user's URL request to deliver the correct content. An example of using a mod_redirect is when content has been moved to another location and requires a new URL. A user may ask for Page A and the web server lets the user know their page request is being redirected to Page B, and provides an HTTP code explaining the reason for the redirect. An example of using mod_rewrite is when you're going to simplify the URL structure internally to eliminate long URLs that are often the product of database-driven websites (i.e., the URLs are not informative or easy for users to remember).

A good way to distinguish these two functions from one another is that mod _redirects are *external* communication between the user and *your* web server informing them that *you* are making a change to their request and providing the reason. The key thing to note is that a mod_redirect is an external, transparent (i.e., trustworthy) communication that explains your actions and does not hide anything from the user.

A mod_rewrite is an *internal* communication between *your* web server and *your* web application to change the user's request. The user is never informed that *you* have decided to change their request. As you can imagine, mod_rewrite can be abused to trick users, and is often used by "black hat" SEOs. If your staff or SEO consultant decide to use a mod_rewrite make sure the same content is served to every user every time. Serving different content for the same URL request, without informing the user, is a violation of most search engine policies and your domain will be penalized and possibly banned.

Search engines test and enforce their policies very rigorously to keep trust high with their customers. Recently, Google's own Chrome division outsourced a marketing campaign to a consulting firm that violated Google's policies. When Googler Matt Cutts's Search Quality team discovered the violation they penalized Google Chrome, moving them from the number 1 position to around the 1,000th position in SERPs, until the violation was corrected (Angotti 2012). The fact that Google doesn't exempt itself from its policies speaks well of the company.

OPTIMIZE SITE STRUCTURE AND NAVIGATION

There is an entire discipline devoted to website design and development, so we won't try to explain what others surely know better than we. But we do think we have a thing or two to offer from the digital repository SEO perspective. Digital repositories usually run on digital asset management (DAM) software, and it is not uncommon for the repositories to be installed on different servers than the institution's overall website, or even its digital library website. There's nothing wrong with this, and from a systems perspective it makes complete sense to not put all your eggs into one basket. But the electronic leaps from one server to another can create a disjointed user experience. Some users may find navigation difficult if a new window is launched to display the repository, rendering the browser's "Back" button useless. Style sheets and designs can be copied to other servers, but it requires a conscious effort initially, and ongoing, coordinated maintenance. Users may also notice if a URL changes in the jump, often from something easy and familiar (e.g., http://lib.utah.edu) to a server named by a systems administrator in honor of his favorite, obscure Egyptian deity, and a URL structure that is complicated by the database running on that server (e.g., http://thoth.library.utah.edu:1701/primo_library/libweb/action/search.do). Finally, jumping from one server to another can make it difficult to gather statistics because website statistical software will usually default to treating different subdomains as silos. It's not always possible, but it makes the most sense to structure sites in terms of domains, subdomains, and directories.

- utah.edu is an example of a domain
- lib.utah.edu is a subdomain
- lib.utah.edu/collections/ represents a directory on that subdomain

The idea is to use the domain and subdomain to organize around a particular institutional product area, and then use the directory structure to organize collections and content within that area. It's a practice that most of us have followed for years when organizing files on our own computers, but the concept sometimes gets lost when we scale up in size and sophistication of our systems. Some DAM and content management system (CMS) vendors have figured out that this strategy makes more sense for users and crawlers, and they use the (internal) mod_rewrite technique described earlier to display shortened URLs rather than the long, query-filled, database-generated URLs.

The bottom line is that the user experience should be the primary motivation for site design. Sites organized by institutional administrative or systems-based structure make no sense at all to users.

OPTIMIZE WEBSITE SPEED

Search engines are obsessed with speed to improve the user experience (Theurer 2006; Brutlag 2009). In 2010 Google officially announced "site speed" was added as a new signal to their search ranking algorithms (Singhal and Cutts 2010). However, most servers and CMS software don't come configured for optimal site speed performance out of the box. For example, only 20 percent of the time a user waits for a page to load is spent actually downloading the HTML document. The other 80 percent of the time is spent making the HTTP request and waiting on the server to respond with the additional components (images, scripts, etc.) to render the page. While reducing the number of web page components is often the easiest performance improvement to make, it's only one of the 35 best practices in 7 categories that Yahoo! recommends you test, optimize, and monitor (Yahoo!). The good news is there are many easy-to-use tools that make improving site speed easy for even the most novice nontechnical web teams. Once again, Google's Analytics Site Speed and Page Speed Insights are good places to start getting general feedback about the performance of your server.

The Yahoo! YSlow and Google Chrome Developer Tools are very powerful and easy-to-use tools. However, the Google Page Speed open source project has a solution that works for virtually every circumstance. The project includes browser extensions for Chrome and Firefox, as well as an online web-based tool that does not require any downloads. They even provide an Apache module—mod_pagespeed—to automatically optimize web pages and resources on your web server, and recently began offering Page Speed Service that does all your site speed optimization without any installs, maintenance, and so on (Google 2012d).

SUMMARY

We've defined search engine-indexing ratio, and identified the most common errors that search engine crawlers experience when they try to harvest content from digital repositories. Understanding those errors, even on a conceptual level, and realizing that they can be addressed are half the battle. Knowing the right team members to whom the task of cleaning up those errors should be delegated is most of the other half.

We've said this before, but it bears repeating: search engines care most about the experience their users will have when they refer those users to your sites. Crawler errors introduced by changes to systems or content can reduce the level of trust search engines have, and can lead to a corresponding reduction in indexing ratio and/or ranking in the SERP. In general you should avoid changing the URLs of your servers and their content, and if you must do so, then do it carefully and with the appropriate redirect messages.

Reducing crawl errors will improve indexing ratios, particularly if your starting point is errors that number in the tens or hundreds of thousands. Higher indexing ratios will lead to increased referrals from search engines, and that in turn will result in more visitors to your sites. And that's really what it's all about.

Chapter Six

Targeting Your Audience

We've talked a lot about how search engines work, and how to optimize your systems to eliminate barriers that might prevent them from harvesting and indexing your digital repositories. Let's talk now about optimizing your content so that your target audience has the best chance of finding it when they search the Internet. This too falls under the theme of search engine optimization, but really you might think of it as content optimization, and it requires knowing a little about the terminology users employ when they go to a search engine. In this chapter we'll talk about keyword analysis, which involves making commonly searched keywords and phrases visible and accessible on your websites. Figuring out what those keywords and phrases should be is the interesting part, but we'll also talk about structuring HTML pages and how to position those carefully selected keywords, marketing through social media sites, and using metadata to your best advantage.

KEYWORDS AND PHRASES

While controlled vocabularies may work well in an organized discipline that has its own indexes and search mechanisms, the Internet is an unruly place where common language rules. Keywords, for better or worse, are what most searchers use to find what they are looking for, and if you want your digital objects to be found you have to work with that reality. Which words might attract high traffic? As usual, Google provides a useful tool to figure out which search keywords and phrases are most popular for any given content. It's called the Google Keyword Tool, and it can help identify words and phrases, compare demand between terms, see related terms, and find new terms and ideas (Britton 2011; Google 2012a). The Google Keyword Tool can also reveal other interesting things. Not only does it help you figure out which keywords would be most useful to describe the contents of your repository, but it can also tell you what it already thinks your site is about based on an analysis of the visible text and how the site is structured. When we first applied the Keyword Tool to the Mountain West Digital Library we were stunned to find that it thought the site was about colleges and universities in the western United States. But then we realized it made sense because we had an extensive list of partners (mostly colleges and universities) smack dab in the middle of the page. If Google thinks a site is about colleges and universities, then it's less likely to direct users there who are looking for digital library collections.

The Keyword Tool will also tell you how often a particular term is searched in a given month, and poking around a bit with this can be eye-opening. For instance, it turns out there's really not much point in calling what you've created a "digital collection." Why? Almost nobody searches that phrase. At the time of this writing global searches of "digital collection" were occurring only 590 times per month. "Digital library" was being searched 12,100 times. And "online library" was being searched 22,200 times. Numbers like that make it obvious which phrase to use, but the exercise also points out how insular the language of a profession or discipline can become. The Google Keyword Tool helps us to understand the language used by the rest of the world.

Keyword idea generation and the targeting process can get very sophisticated and expensive, with online merchants estimating the expected revenue and return on investment of a visitor based upon the visitor's search terms and referral engine, but we are only going to provide collection managers with some general direction to get started. Begin your keyword analysis by using the Keyword Tool to identify "broad" keyword terms and phrases with high traffic volume. Make note of "high-" and "low-"competition keywords to get an idea of the level of effort required to rank well in SERPs. If the collection URL is new, or your institution has a relatively small Internet presence, you should get started by targeting the "low"-competition keywords and phrases. Between 25 percent and 30 percent of the searches conducted use a single keyword (Tatham 2011; Keyword Discovery 2011). However, focusing your attention on any single keyword is a mistake due to a phenomenon called the "long-tail of search," named after how keyword search data appears when graphed. The top keywords that users search for represent a very small portion of the total search traffic (see figures 6.1, 6.2, and 6.3) (Fishkin and Tancer 2009a; Fishkin and Tancer 2009b; Fishkin and Tancer 2009c). The long-tail phenomenon is compounded by the fact that "user click though" percentages increase with the number of words a search engine user types into the search box (Keyword Discovery 2011). In other words, users who search by single terms are less likely to click through to a specific page or repository item.

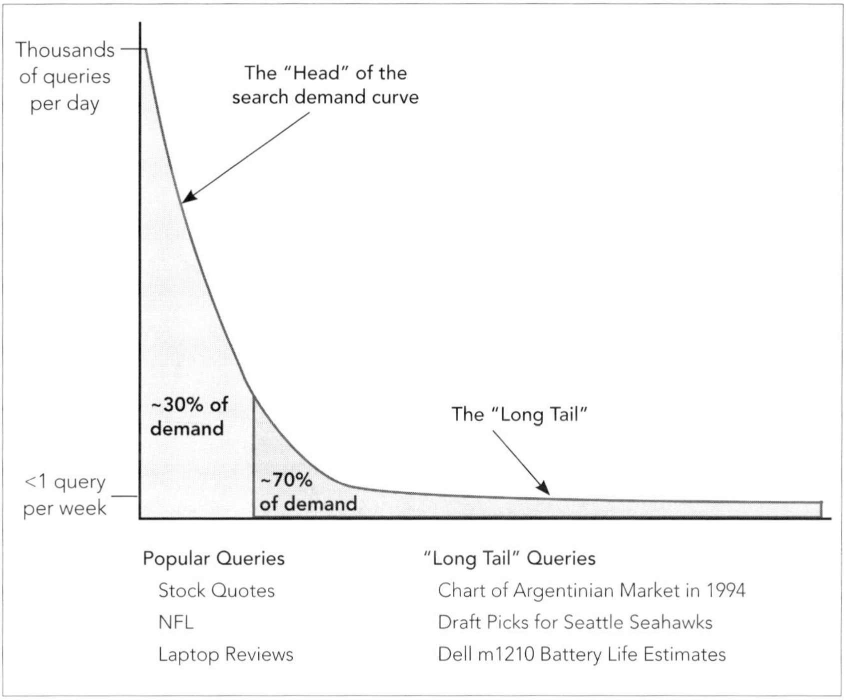

FIGURE 6.1
Search Engine Keyword Demand

The top thousand most searched for keywords on the Internet (the "head") produced about 10 percent of the search traffic, the next nine thousand (the "chunky body") produced about 18 percent of total search traffic, and the remaining search traffic was contained in a long and unpredictable tail of keywords. One researcher described the data by saying "if search were represented by a tiny lizard with a one-inch head, the tail of that lizard would stretch for 221 miles" (Tancer 2008).

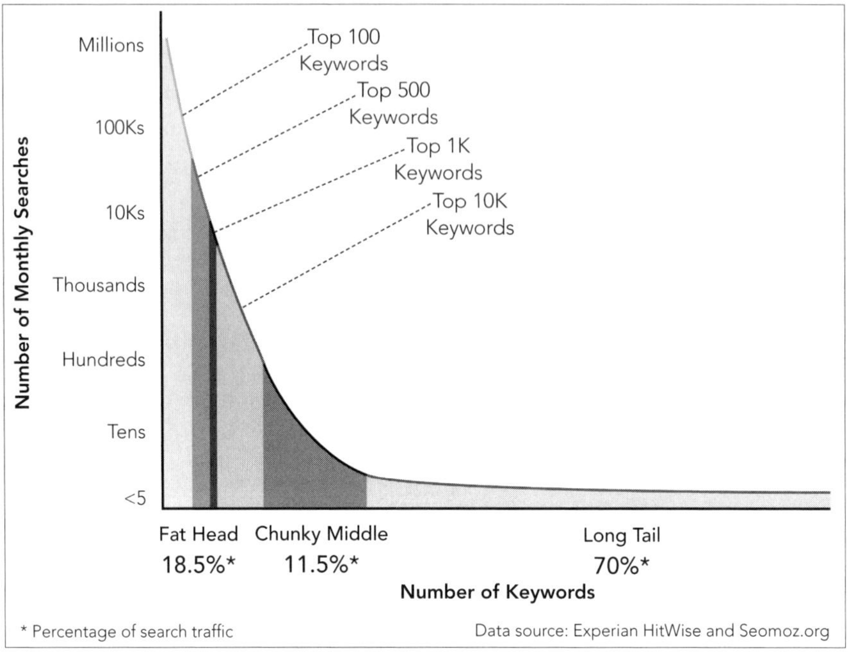

FIGURE 6.2
The Search Demand Curve

Competition is a metric used by the Google Keyword Tool that lets you know how difficult it is to rank well in SERPs. "High"-competition keyword terms and phrases have a great deal of economic value due to the potential revenue users might generate when searching for the keyword term or phrase.

> Google wants to improve its SERPs with websites creating "great content and great websites." Google is introducing an over-optimization penalty to "level the playing field" by giving websites with great content but limited budgets for SEO experts a better chance of ranking well in SERPs (Schwartz 2012a)

The Western Waters Digital Library was created to provide a resource about historical water issues in the western United States. "Water supply" and "water quality" turn out to be very good phrases to include in the website and repository

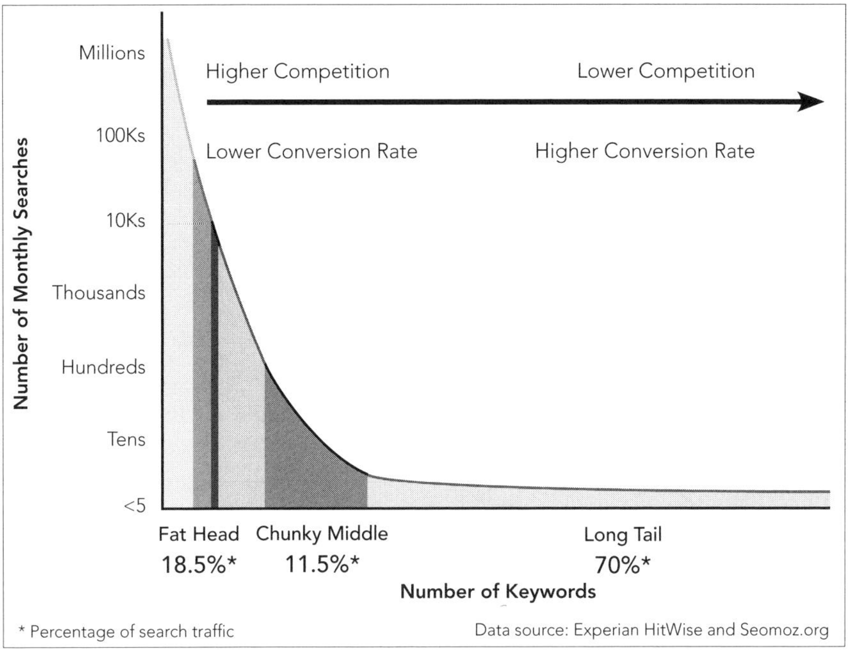

FIGURE 6.3
The Search Demand Curve Competition Conversion

metadata, as each draws approximately 300,000 global searches per month and there is low competition for both. "Whitewater" is another potential search term that comes to mind when considering this digital library, because many of the images are of river rafting. While "whitewater" is a relatively high-volume, "low"-competition keyword according to the Google Keyword Tool, "rafting" and "whitewater rafting" are very high-volume and high-competition phrases. This is primarily because the people searching these more competitive keyword phrases might spend money on planning a rafting trip or purchasing equipment. Businesses want to convert these Internet users into paying customers and they have considerably more resources than libraries to ensure anyone using the phrase "whitewater rafting" and its derivatives sees their web pages in SERPs first. Having this knowledge should cause collection managers to think twice before using "rafting" in close proximity to "whitewater" to describe this collection. A better strategy for libraries or archives is to start by finding similar high-volume keyword phrases that do not seem to have a great deal of commercial value.

Make It Visible

Once you have keywords and phrases selected you need to consider where to place them. Invisible text on a web page is generally considered taboo since "it presents information to search engines differently than to visitors" and it can "cause your site to be perceived as untrustworthy" (Stamoulis 2010). There are several ways to hide text, including using white text on a white background or setting the font size to zero, but these methods are unacceptable because they're viewed as trying to trick the search engine and its users.

Another kind of text that is invisible to users is meta tags, and these are acceptable to search engines and can be useful, too. Meta tags appear within the opening and closing <head> tags of the HTML underlying the page, and should always include a descriptive title <title> and a description <description> tag that are unique to the page (see the next section). Meta tags may also include creator, date, and keywords, among others, but the usefulness of these tags as a ranking signal for most search engines is debatable. The browser displays only the title tag text in its title bar; the text in other tags remains unseen by the user. Meta tags approximate Dublin Core tags and that works well in most cases, but we'll talk later about institutional repositories, where the use of Dublin Core is not advised. Caution must be exercised in the use of meta tags to avoid a phenomenon called "keyword stuffing" (Wikipedia 2012), in which keywords are repeated randomly. Search engines have grown wise to such attempts and have developed sophisticated algorithms that penalize web pages that have been stuffed with keywords or have been overly optimized. A careful and measured approach to keywords and SEO in general is much more effective. Our advice is to provide text that speaks to the collection or object target audience(s), informs the users about the item, and generally improves users' experiences by helping them determine if the item contains the information they seek. It's helpful to remember that library patrons who visit a reference desk sometimes lack the terminology or knowledge necessary to describe what they are looking for. The true power of SEO is using common terminology that introduces and educates users about your repository's subject matter and its contents.

SEO-FRIENDLY WEB PAGES

This book isn't specifically about SEO for websites, but websites are important "wrappers" for repositories, and we can offer a few pointers for their development that will help improve the user experience and, thus, search engine indexing and visibility. As we've mentioned before, digital objects reside in databases, and the display of the objects occurs when the application pulls what it needs from the database and merges it with some cookie-cutter HTML to display a web page. Since search engines index by triggering the display of website pages from the database and then "reading" what's on those pages, it's important to get at least the following on-page items right. This section assumes you know a little about HTML, and most of it is simply good web practice that will benefit users (especially visually impaired users) as well as search engines.

Title—providing useful text in the Title <title> tag that describes the digital object displayed on the web page is probably the single most important thing you can do. Like a book, article, or movie title, your title communicates a great deal of information about your web page content. Search engines will typically use the title tag text as the first line for each entry on the SERP and it will also function as the link to your content. This means that title tag text should be unique, descriptive, and succinct. Since your web pages are generated dynamically, the results typically will end up on a template that is used over and over by the database. If you're using a content management system or digital asset management system that has been developed without this knowledge, that template will have the same nondescript default text in its title tag that shows up each time a web page is generated. This redundant title is pretty useless as far as users and search engine are concerned (see figure 6.4, "Redundant Title"). Don't despair—your programmer can help. Get him or her to write a script that automatically populates the HTML title tag from the metadata title field (e.g., DC.title) in your database each time the template is used.

Description—the Description tag <description> is typically no longer used as a signal for ranking in SERPs. However, most search engines use the text in the description tag to populate that little blurb that appears under the website title in the SERP (SEW Staff 2007). Having your targeted keywords in the page description tag may help improve user click-through from SERPs if the search engine, such as Google, highlights the user's search terms (see figure 6.5, "Page Description").

Internal Link Structure—like a book's table of contents, organize your menus and folders around the "reader" and ensure you include the

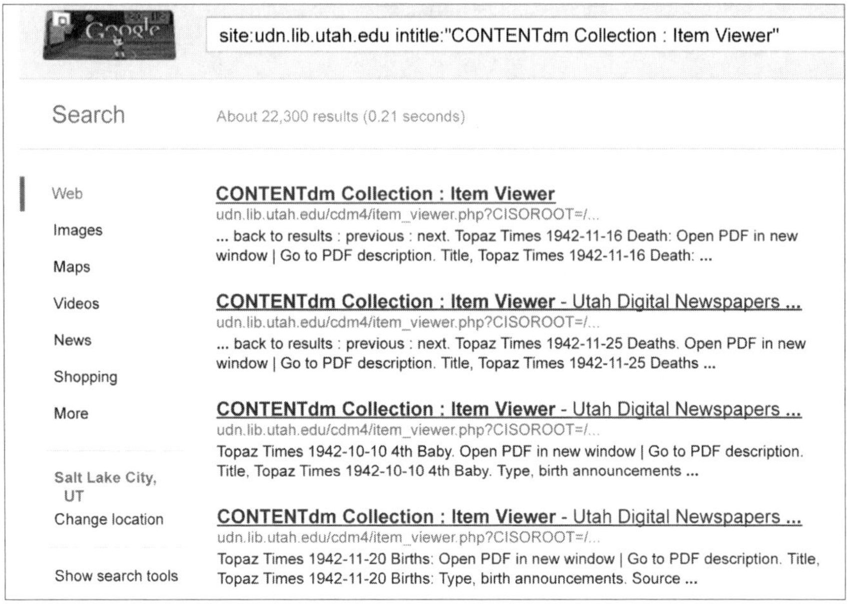

FIGURE 6.4
Redundant Title

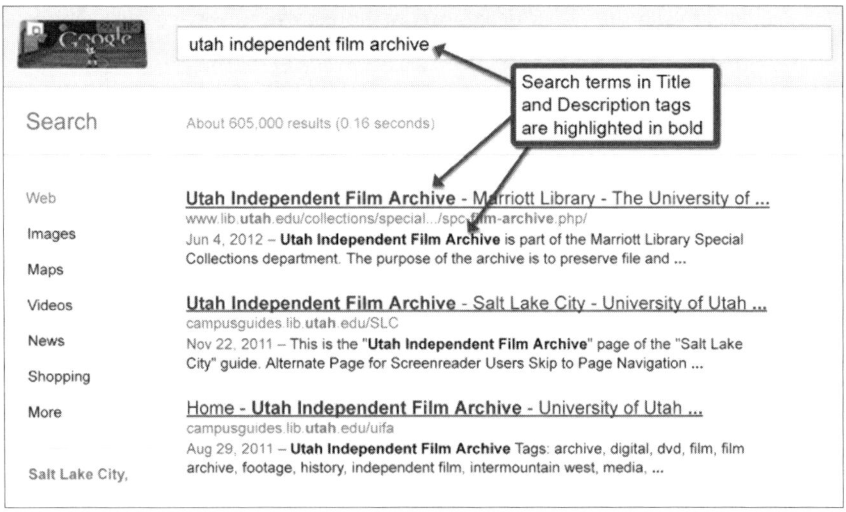

FIGURE 6.5
Page Description

broad keyword terms you want to target in the text between the link tag <a href=>. Your decisions about organizing and naming internal link structure play a very important role in the user experience and include strong signals that search engines use to help establish the context and importance of your web pages. Consider your external users (students, researchers, and so on) and how they would best understand your collection organization. For example, an IR might provide two top-level menu schemas from the home page: one allows the user to browse the IR collection by colleges and departments; and the other, chronologically. Do not confuse the reader by including top-level menu schemas to browse rarely used perspectives. Researchers rarely start their search by paper type (i.e., dissertation, journal article, preprint, and so on). These atypical menu schemas should be considered like a book's appendixes; it's nice to have when you want them but should not be considered equal to the book's chapters.

Out-bound Links—like references cited in a book, collection managers should also pay considerable attention to the out-bound links they choose to include on a page, as well as the text they use to describe them. Remember that out-bound links to other websites are a "vote" about their relevance to your web page's content. Do not dilute your vote or confuse the message by including too many out-bound links that are similar or redundant. Also, ensure each out-bound link points to an authority you trust on the topic and adds value by helping the user identify additional information related to the page (i.e., targeted keywords). It's also important to use clear, descriptive, and relevant text to describe the out-bound link—never use "click here" as hyperlink text.

Headings—HTML is a structured markup language, and heading tags (<h1>, <h2>, <h3>, etc.) imply hierarchy. Like an outline, heading tags can help organize your page content, and text entered into the tags seems to provide a small signal that search engines find useful for indexing and ranking purposes.

Accessibility—the <alt> tag is used to name and describe images and is a very important signal for search engines, not only because it's good for visually impaired users, but also because search engines can't read images without associated text, either.

Body Text—this is the area between the opening and closing <body> tags in the HTML code, and represents the majority of the content a user sees in her client browser. Descriptive text in this area should provide details about the object using language and keywords consistent with the other page tags described above.

Just like a well-written book, a page title, description, headings, images, and body text should tell a story using consistent terminology and vocabulary. The references included by the author (i.e., external links) should have authority and trust to aid the user in getting more information on the topic. The table of contents (i.e., internal link structure) should help the user understand what the author thinks is important and help them easily navigate to the page with the information they seek.

BUILDING COMMUNITY SUPPORT WITH LINKS

In this chicken-and-egg world, websites that are valued by users and linked from numerous other websites will also be valued by search engines and placed highly in rankings. Achieving one before the other is the hard part. Earning community support takes communication and cooperation, but there are things you can do to make the process easier. First, create a short description for each of your collections. Ensure that they contain the high-volume keyword phrases determined relevant to your target audience. The general collection description should contain both "high"-competition and "low"-competition keywords and phrases. Next, identify the people and organizations that could be supporters and request that they link back to your collection using the short general description you created. These might be other libraries or archives in a regional network. You should also ask them for a "deep-link" to specific pages in your collection that are highly relevant to them, and you should be prepared to do the same for them if appropriate. Post information about your collection and the pages that relate to specific topics of interest on social media sites and get interested parties to comment on them (more on social media in the next section).

Another very powerful marketing mechanism is getting your library or institution to issue official press releases about specific collections. National newspapers and other media outlets often pick up press releases, and getting a mention in those outlets will reach far larger audiences than you could hope for on your own; we've seen large and sustained spikes in visitation after a particular page was linked to by the news media. Official press releases are usually handled by an institution's marketing or public affairs department, but try to be involved in the process so that the targeted keywords, descriptions, and collection links you've developed are included.

KEEPING IT FRESH WITH SOCIAL MEDIA

Social media are one area where Google is not the dominant player, but that doesn't mean it should be discounted. Things can change quickly. MySpace was the first significant social media site, but it ceded its position to Facebook years ago, and while Google+ has only a fraction of Facebook's market share, it's quickly gaining ground (Angotti 2011). Regardless of which of the top sites has the most market share, it's clear that social media in general are heavily used and that the sites have a strong presence in search engine indexes. Even LinkedIn, Pinterest, Twitter, and YouTube, while arguably not all pure social media sites, draw huge traffic volumes (Kitt 2012). A farsighted marketing strategy should include a presence for digital libraries that are trying to increase visitation.

Every library should have a Facebook and/or Google+ page, but they come with responsibility for upkeep. An outdated page doesn't help marketing efforts and may even hurt them. Using social media effectively means someone has to be assigned to lead the effort, and a strategy that outlines intended audience, team responsibilities, and tone is helpful for success. Communication styles and expectations vary from one social media outlet to another. Twitter is unique in its 140-character limit, and the expectation is that numerous tweets will be posted by users who are seized with an idea or are communicating from a conference, but that same frequency of posts will be considered spam on Facebook (Hamasu and Bramble 2012).

There's a fair amount of debate about whether search engines prefer new or updated content, and as is often the case the truth lies somewhere in the middle. Proponents of social media freshness of content for SEO point out that search engines prefer to offer users material that is alive, being updated, viewed, and commented on by users with social authority (i.e., they have followers that read

Google did roll out a new indexing system in 2010 called Caffeine, but the freshness it affects is Google's index itself, by updating it more frequently (Grimes 2010).

their original content). In late 2010 Google made the importance of content "freshness" official by confirming that they are using social media signals to determine the social authority or trust of a web page author or creator in their primary ranking algorithm (Cutts 2010b). This is one of many signals used by search engines and they tend to place more value on the quality of links than the number of links. The freshness quotient can create a challenge for libraries and archives whose content tends to be static and unchanging, but it's still possible to build user groups and conversations around segments of that content. Below are some basic social media strategies we recommend to get started once you have established a web presence that describes your library, its digital collection program, and each digital collection.

Institutionalize Your Social Media

Just as we advised setting up a Google Account and Windows LiveID for creating and administering your Webmaster Tools and Google Analytics, we recommend you set up and associate a shared institutional e-mail address for each social media "brand" you plan to create and maintain. One brand example might be the University of Utah's Institutional Repository "USpace" and another could be the University of Utah Press. Ensure that each "brand" has its own physical mailing address, contact phone number, and URL. For example:

> USpace Institutional Repository
> 295 South 1500 East, Suite 5010
> Salt Lake City, UT 84112
> (801) 585-3101
> uspace@utah.edu

Improve Your Profile Ranking by Laying the Groundwork

Google Places and Bing Business Portal are good places to start for establishing an online brand you plan to build using social media. While these are not necessarily social tools, the verification process is one of the best ways to begin building trust and influencing how the search engines understand your digital repositories.

Wikipedia is the sixth most visited site in the world, and it can be a great source of referrals to your digital collection. Wikipedia has strict "conflict of interest" rules and is no place for self-promotion or marketing. However, we believe libraries and their digital collection programs do warrant some article space and references that Wikipedia users will value. Start by identifying your organization's Wikipedia entry and suggest some facts about your digital collection programs via the "Talk" tab (a.k.a., "Discussion"). It is very important to follow Wikipedia etiquette and not make any edits directly to articles about your library or digital collections. Not everyone has good intentions like you do (Sernovitz 2007). You should also look for topics related to your individual digital collections and provide some facts on the topics that reference your collection as a source. Again, use the "Talk" tab to make suggestions to the article editors for content that users will value. This process may play out in the following example: a Wikipedia article about the Studebaker car company includes a photograph of a Studebaker horse-drawn carriage from 1908, pulled from a collection owned by the Utah State Historical Society (USHS). There is a link back to the USHS, and that provides credibility to the repository domain because of Wikipedia's editorial vetting process and its status as a trusted hub. This kind of repurposing and reuse of content is also consistent with the missions of libraries and archives, even if it happens outside the domains of those organizations. This is a useful metric that may be difficult to measure, but it will play into our discussion of funding models in chapter 8.

Facebook and Google+—keep your page fresh by announcing new additions to the collection and provide short, informative articles with direct links to the relevant digital objects in your repository. Use the relevant keyword terms that you discovered earlier in the chapter with the Keyword Tool for the collection or digital objects in the announcement. Some social media site managers recommend using dashboard software, like Hootsuite or Klout, to manage multiple social media sites, analyze traffic, and schedule messages, and they make these further recommendations (Hamasu and Bramble 2012):

- Post around 9 a.m., the most popular time of the day for social media
- Leave at least two hours between posts
- Engage users by asking open-ended questions
- Share events, milestones, and celebrations

WHICH METADATA SCHEMAS SHOULD YOU USE?

Metadata schemas are powerful frameworks for organizing content, and libraries have long used them to describe their holdings (think MARC). Numerous schemas exist for academic disciplines: CDWA is used for art, Darwin Core for biology, EML for ecology, DDI for social sciences, and so on. Dublin Core is probably the most heavily used schema in digital libraries, and it is perfectly adequate for many applications, but the problem with any metadata schema is that most website developers don't use any at all, and search engines can't count on the metadata being applied consistently in those that do. The result is that general-purpose search engines like Google tend not to use the metadata even where it is applied appropriately.

Some specialty engines, like Google Scholar, do make extensive use of metadata, but as we'll see in the next chapter, Google Scholar wants metadata schemas that can express bibliographic citations specifically and accurately, which Dublin Core does not do very well.

Since search engines crawl the web pages that are generated from databases (rather than crawling the databases themselves), your carefully applied metadata inside the database will not even be seen by search engines unless you write scripts to display the metadata tags and their values in HTML meta tags. It is crucial to understand that any metadata offered to search engines must be recognizable as part of a schema and must be machine-readable, which is to say that the search engine must be able to parse the metadata accurately. For example, if you enter a bibliographic citation into a single metadata field the search engine probably won't know how to distinguish the article title from the journal title, or the volume from the issue number. In order for the search engine to read those citations effectively each part of the citation must have its own field. Making sure metadata is machine-readable requires patterns and consistency, which will also prepare it for transformation to other schema. This is far more important than picking any single metadata schema.

The Semantic Web, Structured Data, and Schema.org.

We invest a great deal of time and money creating digital collections, and we usually create web pages that describe the collection's purpose, what it contains, its contributors, and so on, to give visitors some context they can use to understand the collection. We also take great pains in creating metadata that describe each object in the collection to give it meaning and allow users to reference or discuss the item. While humans can understand and associate the concepts they read, search engines have a very limited capacity for interpreting the meaning of the information we so painstakingly provide.

To help search engines understand the context and meaning of our digital objects we must provide structure to our content using additional tags in our HTML. These tags will say to search engines directly, for example, "this information describes a specific digital object as a scholarly paper, written by an author who works at an academic institution, published by an organization on a certain date." Sounds easy enough, but communicating with a machine requires an up-front agreement on the specific language and precise vocabulary being used to communicate. The word "bloody" has very different meanings to a person raised in the United States and a person raised in the United Kingdom. Search engines do not understand the regional variations, sarcasm, humor, hand gestures, facial expressions, body language, tone of voice, inflection, and so on that humans rely on heavily to communicate meaning.

Enter schema.org. In 2011 Google, Bing, Yandex (the largest Russian search engine), and Yahoo! "joined forces to create a common set of schemas for structured data markup on web pages" with the aim of helping search engines to better understand websites (Goel and Gupta 2011). Originally, schema.org was planned to use only HTML microdata (Hickson 2011) as the mechanism, or language for implementing schema.org structured data vocabularies. But it has also recently added support for RDFa as an alternative "language" that developers using "RDF-based tools and Linked Data" can use to implement the schema.org vocabulary (danbri 2011). While it's not our intent to fully discuss schema.org, microdata, or linked data here, we do think it's important for repository managers (and especially catalogers) to be cognizant of these developments because they hold great promise for fulfilling the potential of the semantic web. Sites that already offer microdata provide a great benefit to Google's users through its "rich snippets," which display additional details about web pages in the search results (Fox 2009). Another example of Google's use of microdata appears in its "recipe search," where metadata about recipes provide a faceted navigational search (Fox 2011). If Google can do this for recipes, imagine what it could do for library digital repositories that already have rich metadata describing the objects. The bridge that will get that rich metadata to be understood by search engines is the techniques recommended by schema.org, and putting those techniques into place in digital repositories is the responsibility of librarians and archivists.

SUMMARY

This chapter has described how to appropriately represent the content of your repositories for searchers. Selecting descriptive keywords and phrases is the first step, and it's a different ball game in the SEO world than it has been for traditional library indexes. HTML tags play a critical role in organizing information to help users understand what they are seeing in their web browser or hearing in their screen reader. Collection managers and catalogers should spend considerable time in ensuring that objects within their collection have unique, descriptive, and relevant text, and IT staff should help them make sure that text is discoverable and usable by search engines and users. Taking the time to craft the text using specific keywords and phrases within each page's title, description, heading, and body tags used to give structure to your page is time and effort well spent because it will improve the user's experience and provide search engines with more information to make decisions about index inclusion and placement in SERPs. Employing basic publicity and marketing techniques in traditional as well as newer social media outlets to help make repository sites known can pay off in increased indexing and visitation.

In the next chapter we'll look at a specific case of a specialty search engine—Google Scholar—that has become very popular with faculty researchers and graduate students, and how it is having difficulty indexing the contents of many institutional repositories.

Chapter Seven

Google Scholar and Institutional Repositories

At some point in our research it became apparent that our institutional repository (IR) had a very low indexing ratio in Google Scholar (GS). Okay, it was worse than that: our IR, named USpace, had an indexing ratio in GS that was less than 1 percent. Everything we'd been doing to raise the indexing ratio of our digital collections had been tremendously effective, and one year after beginning our SEO work we had achieved a 98 percent Google indexing ratio for our IR collections. But in GS they remained near zero.

IRs were developed to manage and ensure long-term access to academic research publications, and GS was created as a search engine for those publications whether they reside in IRs, at publisher repositories, or other research-oriented sites. We knew that GS was indexing publisher repositories because we could see content from those publishers in search results, and we came to believe the reasons for the low indexing ratio of IRs stem mostly from the metadata requirements of GS. These requirements differ significantly from the practices of most IRs, and they

The University of Utah Marriott Library implemented most of the recommendations contained within this chapter in September 2012. As of December 2012, the University of Utah has increased the number of primary links to its scholarly papers in Google Scholar from 422 to approximately 2,650—a 525% increase. This includes more than 1,900 direct links to PDFs with more papers being added each week.

were only made public in 2010 at GS's Webmaster Inclusion Guidelines website (Google Scholar 2011b).

In this chapter we will describe a survey we conducted in 2011 that showed that the problem of low indexing ratios of IRs in GS is widespread. We will also discuss three pilot projects that we conducted with a subset of our IR data to test our hypothesis that altering repository metadata schema to a schema recommended by GS would improve our indexing ratio.

GOOGLE AND GOOGLE SCHOLAR

Google and Google Scholar are separate indexes, and GS has a different focus from its much larger parent. Anurag Acharya, GS's founding engineer, has stated that the goal is to offer the "most comprehensive list of research papers available on the web," and that GS limits its results to "peer reviewed papers, theses, books, abstracts, and technical reports" (Assisi 2005). More recently, GS has added patents and legal cases to the items it indexes. For several years after its launch in 2004 GS wasn't considered a serious source for researchers, but in more recent years it has significantly increased its scholarly content, and its use by faculty researchers and graduate students has also increased (Rieger 2009; Mikki 2009; Herrera 2010; Haglund

A peculiarity of GS's presentation of academic papers is that it offers links directly to the PDF document. This is expedient for users as it gets them directly to the content, but it also strips any context that may have been provided by the repository's HTML display. In other words, metadata, institutional logos, and other information normally included in display templates are lost unless they are inserted into the PDF itself. The practice can also affect the reporting of visitation statistics through website analytics software that utilizes page tagging, like the Google Analytics tracking code that we discussed in chapter 4. Separating the PDF file from the HTML display means that the visit will not be counted because the tracking code is not executed when the PDF is called directly. This problem can by overcome by having the web server execute a PHP script containing the tracking code before serving the requested PDF, but it is unlikely that many repository managers are doing this, or are even aware that their visitation and download statistics may be underreported as a result of GS's item display practice.

and Olsson 2008; McKay 2007). GS has its own crawlers that visit IRs and publisher repositories, among others, to harvest content appropriate for its index.

OPEN ACCESS AND INSTITUTIONAL REPOSITORIES

The open access movement was launched to improve access to publicly funded research, and to give libraries some leverage against the rampant inflation in journal subscription prices. Institutional repositories were one product of this movement; they capture the intellectual output of the faculty, staff, and students of universities or academic disciplines and assure perpetual and free access to that output. IRs often include electronic theses and dissertations (ETDs), and most are managed by academic libraries or scholarly societies. Over the past decade IRs have enjoyed advances and suffered setbacks, but through the consistent work of many individuals at numerous institutions they are achieving enough mass to become viable sources of research publications. They also hold the promise of contributing significantly to author citation rates. Research in the United Kingdom suggests that institutional repositories may play a crucial role in measuring research output, and in turn may affect university rankings (Key Perspectives Ltd. and Brown 2009). The *Times Higher Education* publishes an annual ranking of the top world universities, and research citations contribute 32.5 percent toward each university's score (Times Higher Education 2010).

Libraries have not developed a mechanism to aggregate and search IRs, and thus GS has become the best de facto free search engine available for IR content. But just as institutional repositories are gaining enough mass to make them useful and credible sources of research output, the difficulties associated with SEO threaten to undermine their potential. Faculty and other authors who contribute publications to institutional repositories may lose interest if their publications can't be located (and cited) in academically oriented search engines like GS or Microsoft's Academic Search.

USPACE

The University of Utah Institutional Repository (USpace) was launched in 2005 on CONTENTdm, the digital asset management software that we use for the vast majority of our digital collections. USpace currently contains approximately

12,000 items, most of which are separated into collections for scholarly papers, electronic theses and dissertations, and institutional archives. When we first revealed USpace's indexing ratio woes, many in the library pressed us to migrate to another IR software, but we argued that the real problem lay in our data set and in GS's requirements. While earlier versions of CONTENTdm did have some SEO barriers, most of those were eliminated in version 6, which separated the user interface from the database. Successfully raising USpace's indexing ratio to 98 percent in Google's main index while we were still running version 5.x proved this point rather conclusively.

SURVEYS OF IR AND THEIR INDEXING RATIOS IN GOOGLE SCHOLAR

Unfortunately, GS does not offer the same kind of Webmaster Tools as its parent organization, so it's difficult to determine indexing ratio of IRs. IR managers who want an approximate reading of their indexing ratios in GS are left with relatively labor-intensive manual options, like searching for known items by their titles and ensuring that the items found are from the URL in question. To determine whether the problem of poor indexing is widespread we decided to conduct a survey similar to the one we had done of the Mountain West Digital Library repositories. This method is, of course, slow and laborious, but it is relatively accurate, allowing articles to be counted whether they appear in an initial list of results in GS or are hidden behind the "versions" link

We identified seven IRs through the Directory of Open Access Repositories, also known as OpenDOAR (University of Nottingham 2011). We chose them for their academic content and to represent several of the more common repository software types: DSpace, Digital Commons, EPrints, Fedora, and IR+. We first created a data set for each repository by using crawler software to harvest titles from that repository. This method mimicked Internet search engine crawlers, and we gathered between 500 and 1,500 article titles from each repository and saved them into Excel spreadsheets. Using a sampling methodology developed for verifying database backups (LaRock 2010), we randomized those titles and searched forty from each set by pasting the article titles into the GS search box. We used Zotero to create metadata records and snapshots for each search result, whether we found the article or not. "Versions" links were followed whenever found, and we also captured those results as a snapshot attached to the same metadata record in Zotero.

Of the seven repositories that we sampled, three showed very high indexing ratios (88 percent to 98 percent), while the other four showed ratios below 50 percent (see figure 7.1). A discussion about the reasons for these differences follows.

DRAWING CONCLUSIONS FROM THE SURVEYS

Data from the survey reveal a matrix of issues, and even generating the data set proved difficult. Because we used crawler software to harvest article titles, we encountered many of the same basic navigational problems that search engine crawlers face when trying to harvest institutional repositories. These problems can include websites that throw up design barriers such as frames, JavaScripts, or image-heavy sites that offer little indexable text. Another problem is that some repositories mix the scholarly content that GS wants with content (such as historical photographs) in which it has no interest. We compiled the guidelines shown in figure 7.1 from stated recommendations at GS's Webmaster Inclusion Guidelines website (Google Scholar 2011b), and they include recommendations to facilitate crawler navigation on the site and for metadata. Although Google Scholar did not mention the use of sitemaps or sitemap indexes, we checked them because they are an important SEO best practice.

GS's indexing recommendations state that repositories should offer crawlers (and users) the ability to navigate all content chronologically as well as showing only papers that were recently added. PDF files of the papers should be less than ten clicks from the home page (fewer clicks is even better) and an absolute URL to the PDF file should be present. Appropriately configured sitemap indexes and robots.txt files are also recommended. The most validating differences in terms of metadata were found in those repositories that used one of the GS-recommended schemas (bepress, Highwire Press, PRISM, or EPrints) in the meta tags of HTML pages. Those repositories that did not make their metadata available in one of those publisher schemas in the HTML meta tags

> The point about metadata being expressed in HTMl meta tags is a crucial one, and we'll demonstrate how this is done later in the chapter. For now, it's important to understand that metadata using one of the recommended schemas does no good at all if those tags are buried in the database; they have to appear in the HTML display template of each paper to be useful to crawlers.

	Cornell	Oregon	Cal Tech	Texas A&M Faculty	UW Aquatic Tech Reports	Columbia	Rochester
Indexing ratio	98%	88%	88%	48%	46%	45%	38%
Software	Digital Commons	DSpace	ePrints	DSpace	DSpace	Digital Commons	IR+
Titles available/ captured	Unknown /1,421	4,067/ 1,463	24,146 /1,306	763/757	563/539	3,819/ 1,432	1,562/926
Crawling							
Browse by date	No	Yes	Yes	Yes	Yes	No	No
Recently added	No	No	Yes	No	No	No	No
10 clicks from home page	Yes	Yes	Yes	No, only first 200	No, only first 200	Yes	No
Robots.txt	Yes	Yes, not in root	Yes	Yes, disallows browse by date	Yes, disallows browse by date	Yes, not configured	Yes
Sitemapindex	Yes	No	No	Yes, not compliant with standards	No	No	No
Indexing							
Meta tag schema in HTML headers	bepress	DC	ePrints & DC	None	DC & DCTERMS	None	None
Title	Yes	Yes	Yes	No	Yes	No	No
Author	Yes	Yes	Yes	No	Yes	No	No
Pub date	Yes	Yes	Yes	No	DCTERMS	No	No
Publisher	Yes	Yes	Yes	No	No	No	No
Journal	No	No	Yes	No	No	No	No
Volume	No	No	Yes	No	No	No	No
Issue	No	No	Yes	No	No	No	No
First page	No	No	Yes	No	No	No	No
Last page	No	No	Yes	No	No	No	No
Absolute URL to PDF	Yes	Yes	Yes	No	No	No	No
Institution	n/a	n/a	n/a	n/a	n/a	No	n/a
Dissertation name	n/a	n/a	n/a	n/a	n/a	No	n/a

FIGURE 7.1
Google Scholar Indexing Ratio of Seven Institutional Repositories

> "*If you're a university repository,* we recommend that you use the latest version of Eprints (eprints.org), Digital Commons (digitalcommons.bepress.com), or DSpace (dspace.org) software to host your papers. If you use a less common hosting product or service, or an older version of these, please read the rest of this document and make sure that your website meets our technical guidelines" (Google Scholar 2011b).

generally fared much more poorly than those that did. In general, IRs that followed GS guidelines and recommendations had a much higher indexing ratio than sites that did not.

GS makes specific recommendations for IR software on its Inclusion Guidelines for Webmasters site (see sidebar), but our survey demonstrates that software makes little or no difference; the problem cuts across institutions, repository focus, and repository software. Instead, indexing ratio success has much more to do with how carefully a repository follows the guidelines described above. While IR software can be built to include the GS recommendations (and some are), developers have little control over how the software is implemented at a local site. A well-designed IR software may be undermined by a simple robots.txt file that isn't configured correctly, or by a poorly designed website that creates barriers to crawlers. Hosted software, also referred to as software-as-a service, can eliminate these local mistakes, but they are sometimes beyond the price point of libraries or scholarly societies.

WHY DUBLIN CORE METADATA DOESN'T WORK VERY WELL

As we mentioned in chapter 1, GS announced on its Webmaster Inclusion Guidelines site in 2010: "Use Dublin Core tags (e.g., DC.title) as a last resort—they work poorly for journal papers" (Google Scholar 2011a). Although Dublin Core is recognized to be a standard of the lowest common denominator, libraries have used it widely for most digital repositories, including IRs. The Dublin Core schema works "poorly for journal papers" because it does not include adequate fields for citation data and because it is interpreted inconsistently. Citation information such as journal name, volume and issue number, and page numbers span of the article is usually entered into a single field, such as DC.Relation or DC.Source in simple Dublin Core, and there is no specified format or consistency. This makes it difficult for a search engine like GS to accurately parse and index the data into their individual bibliographic components, particularly since GS wants to pass on to researchers the ability to quickly and easily download a citation that can be imported into citation management software like BibTeX or EndNote. The Dublin Core Metadata Initiative website (DCMI 2005) does include guidelines for encoding bibliographic citation information using a qualification of the DC.Identifier field (called "bibliographicCitation"), but this is still only a single field. It is also unlikely that many repositories have updated to reflect the relatively recent development of DC Qualifiers. Dublin Core also doesn't facilitate various academic paper types: there is no specific field to distinguish a preprint from a journal article, a book chapter from a book, a working paper from a conference proceeding, or a dissertation. This problem gets to the core of the issue we discussed in the previous chapter, that is, data must be rendered as machine-readable, and libraries and archives don't always do that very well.

The four schemas that GS recommends are more adept at structuring citation data appropriately. Highwire Press, a division of Stanford University, developed its schema for journal articles and GS extended the tags to cover additional academic paper types, such as working papers, dissertations, manuscripts, conference papers, books, and book chapters. We used the extended Highwire Press tags to test the hypothesis that transforming our Dublin Core metadata would lead to an increase in indexing ratio in GS for an IR.

First Pilot Project

Let's cut to the chase. As we mentioned at the beginning of this chapter, our first pilot project on USpace was a great success for getting indexed in Google, but a complete failure for getting indexed in GS. We went from an average indexing ratio of 18.33 percent for our IR collections to a 97.82 percent indexing ratio in Google, but our indexing ratio in GS didn't budge. We won't waste your time explaining the details of everything we did to try to get our IR indexed by GS, except to say that we followed the instructions on the GS Webmaster Inclusion Guidelines website that suggested extending Dublin Core to include specific citation fields so that article citation data could be represented appropriately. Figure 7.2 shows how we extended the Dublin Core tags in our repository to match Highwire Press tags.

Number	Highwire Press Tags	Dublin Core Tags
1	citation_issn	n/a
2	citation_isbn	n/a
3	citation_technical_report_number	n/a
4	citation_title	DC.title
5	citation_keywords	DC.subject
6	citation_conference_title	DC.relation.ispartof
7	citation_journal_title	DC.relation.ispartof
8	citation_publisher	DC.publisher
9	citation_dissertation_institution	DC.publisher
10	citation_technical_report_institution	DC.publisher
11	citation_language	DC.language
12	citation_date	DC.issued
13	citation_pdf_url	DC.identifier
14	citation_author	DC.creator
15	citation_volume	DC.citation.volume
16	citation_firstpage	DC.citation.spage
17	citation_issue	DC.citation.issue
18	citation_lastpage	DC.citation.epage

FIGURE 7.2
Crosswalk of Dublin Core to Highwire Press

Second Pilot Project

During the summer of 2011 we consulted with OCLC and Google Scholar with the aim of developing and testing a second pilot project.

We selected nineteen papers from USpace for the second pilot.

1. Six of seven GS paper types were represented and the full-text PDF document was included for each paper. The book paper type was out of scope for this pilot
   a. Dissertation and Thesis (see figure 7.3)
   b. Conference Article (see figure 7.4)
   c. Working Paper (see figure 7.4)
   d. Manuscript and Preprint (see figure 7.5)
   e. Journal Article (see figure 7.5)
   f. Book Chapter (see figure 7.6)

Number	Meta Tag	PhD	Masters
1	citation_author	Rague, Brian William	Wu, Shangduan
2	citation_date	2010/08	2010/07
3	citation_title	A CS1 pedagogical approach to parallel thinking	Electronic structure and transport property of disordered graphene
4	citation_publisher	Not relevant	Not relevant
5	citation_journal_title	Not relevant	Not relevant
6	citation_volume	Not relevant	Not relevant
7	citation_issue	Not relevant	Not relevant
8	citation_firstpage	1	1
9	citation_lastpage	234	84
10	citation_doi	Not relevant	Not relevant
11	citation_issn	Not relevant	Not relevant
12	citation_isbn	Not relevant	Not relevant
13	citation_keywords	Computer; CS1; Education; Parallel; Programming;	Disorder; Electronic structure; Graphene; Transport property; Electronic structure;
14	citation_dissertation_institution	University of Utah, College of Engineering	University of Utah, College of Science
15	citation_dissertation_name	PhD	MS
16	citation_technical_report_institution	Not relevant	Not relevant
17	citation_technical_report_number	Not relevant	Not relevant
18	citation_language	en	en
19	citation_conference_title	Not relevant	Not relevant
20	citation_inbook_title	Not relevant	Not relevant
21	citation_pdf_url	http://cdm6gs.lib.utah.edu/utils/getfile/collection/uspace/id/5/filename/19.pdf	http://cdm6gs.lib.utah.edu/utils/getfile/collection/uspace/id/0/filename/4.pdf
22	citation_abstract_html_url	http://cdm6gs.lib.utah.edu/cdm/singleitem/collection/uspace/id/5/rec/1	http://cdm6gs.lib.utah.edu/cdm/singleitem/collection/uspace/id/0/rec/1

FIGURE 7.3

Google Scholar Electronic Theses and Dissertations Meta Tags

Number	Meta Tag	Working Paper
1	citation_author	Wolfinger, Nicholas H.; McKeever, Matthew
2	citation_date	2006-07-26
3	citation_title	Thanks for nothing: changes in income and labor force participation for never-married mothers since 1982
4	citation_publisher	Not relevant
5	citation_journal_title	Not relevant
6	citation_volume	
7	citation_issue	
8	citation_firstpage	1
9	citation_lastpage	43
10	citation_doi	
11	citation_issn	Not relevant
12	citation_isbn	Not relevant
13	citation_keywords	Motherhood; Single Mothers; Income; Population surveys
14	citation_dissertation_institution	Not relevant
15	citation_dissertation_name	Not relevant
16	citation_technical_report_institution	Institute of Public & International Affairs (IPIA), University of Utah
17	citation_technical_report_number	2006-07-04
18	citation_language	en
19	citation_conference_title	101st American Sociological Association (ASA) Annual Meeting; 2006 Aug 11-14; Montreal, Canada
20	citation_inbook_title	Not relevant
21	citation_pdf_url	http://cdm6gs.lib.utah.edu/utils/getfile/collection/uspace/id/7/filename/21.pdf
22	citation_abstract_html_url	http://cdm6gs.lib.utah.edu/cdm/single item/collection/uspace/id/7/rec/1

FIGURE 7.4

Google Scholar Working Paper Meta Tags

Number	Meta Tag	Pre-Print	Journal Article
1	citation_author	Maloney, Krisellen; Antelman, Kristin; Arlitsch, Kenning; Butler, John	Maloney, Krisellen; Antelman, Kristin; Arlitsch, Kenning; Butler, John
2	citation_date	2009	2010
3	citation_title	Future leaders' views on organizational culture	Future leaders' views on organizational culture
4	citation_publisher	N/A	Association of College & Research Libraries
5	citation_journal_title	N/A	College and Research Libraries
6	citation_volume		71
7	citation_issue		4
8	citation_firstpage	1	322
9	citation_lastpage	56	347
10	citation_doi		
11	citation_issn		
12	citation_isbn		
13	citation_keywords	Organizational culture	Organizational culture
14	citation_dissertation_institution	Not relevant	Not relevant
15	citation_dissertation_name	Not relevant	Not relevant
16	citation_technical_report_institution	Uspace Institutional Repository, University of Utah	N/A
17	citation_technical_report_number		N/A
18	citation_language	en	en
19	citation_conference_title	Not relevant	Not relevant
20	citation_inbook_title	Not relevant	Not relevant
21	citation_pdf_url	http://cdm6gs.lib.utah.edu/utils/getfile/collection/uspace/id/10/filename/3.pdf	http://cdm6gs.lib.utah.edu/utils/getfile/collection/uspace/id/16/filename/17.pdf
22	citation_abstract_html_url	http://cdm6gs.lib.utah.edu/cdm/singleitem/collection/uspace/id/10/rec/1	http://cdm6gs.lib.utah.edu/cdm/singleitem/collection/uspace/id/16/rec/2

FIGURE 7.5

Google Scholar Pre-Print and Journal Article Meta Tags

Number	Meta Tag	Book Chapter	Book
1	citation_author	Riloff, Ellen M.	Ram, Ashwin
2	citation_date	1999	1999
3	citation_title	Information extraction as a stepping stone toward story understanding	Understanding Language: Understanding Computational Models of Reading
4	citation_publisher	MIT Press	MIT Press
5	citation_journal_title	Not relevant	Not relevant
6	citation_volume	Not relevant	Not relevant
7	citation_issue	Not relevant	Not relevant
8	citation_firstpage	435	1
9	citation_lastpage	460	519
10	citation_issue	Not relevant	Not relevant
11	citation_issue	Not relevant	Not relevant
12	citation_isbn	0-262-18192-4	0-262-18192-4
13	citation_keywords	Information extraction; Story understanding;	Information extraction; Story understanding;
14	citation_dissertation_institution	Not relevant	Not relevant
15	citation_dissertation_name	Not relevant	Not relevant
16	citation_technical_report_institution	Not relevant	Not relevant
17	citation_technical_report_number	Not relevant	Not relevant
18	citation_language	en	en
19	citation_conference_title	Not relevant	Not relevant
20	citation_inbook_title	Understanding Language: Understanding Computational Models of Reading	N/A
21	citation_pdf_url	http://cdm6gs.lib.utah.edu/utils/getfile/collection/uspace/id/9/filename/5.pdf	
22	citation_abstract_html_url	http://cdm6gs.lib.utah.edu/cdm/singleitem/collection/uspace/id/9/rec/1	

FIGURE 7.6
Google Scholar Book and Chapter Meta Tags

Human Readable

McKever, M. & Wolfinger, N.H. (2006). *Thanks for Nothing: Changes in Income and Labor Force Participation for Never-Married Mothers since 1982.* Institute of Public & International Affairs (IPIA), 4, 1–43.

Machine Understandable

```
<meta name="citation_title" content="Thanks for nothing: changes in income
<meta name="citation_author" content="Wolfinger, Nicholas H." />
<meta name="citation_author" content="McKeever, Matthew" />
<meta name="citation_date" content="2006-07-26" />
<meta name="citation_firstpage" content="1" />
<meta name="citation_lastpage" content="42" />
<meta name="citation_keywords" content="Motherhood; Single Mothers; Income
<meta name="citation_technical_report_institution" content="Institute of P
<meta name="citation_technical_report_number" content="2006-07-04" />
<meta name="citation_language" content="en" />
<meta name="citation_conference_title" content="101st American Sociologica
<meta name="citation_pdf_url" content="http://cdm6gs.lib.utah.edu/utils/ge
```

FIGURE 7.7
Human Readable to Machine Understandable Citations

2. Augmented CONTENTdm version 6.0 display templates
    a. Embedded Highwire Press meta tags in the HTML page header of display templates using an automated script (see figure 7.7)
    b. Created a Browse By Year page that provided links to papers in chronological order of publishing date
    c. Created a Recently Added page that listed papers added to the IR within the last thirty days

The second pilot was a moderate success, with 62 percent of papers indexed on the first harvest. However, due to unexpected campus network and power outages that took down the test server for an extended period, the pilot was cut short and GS dropped our server from their index because it was unable to make contact.

Third Pilot Project

For the third and final pilot project, we uploaded fifty-six papers with full-text PDF files and transformed the Dublin Core metadata to Highwire Press tags as described earlier. The same six paper types were represented as before. This time more than 90 percent appeared in the GS index after four weeks. We considered this success to be a significant breakthrough that proved the hypothesis that transforming Dublin Core metadata to a schema that GS recommends will result in much higher indexing ratios.

Transforming Metadata

The thought of manually transforming metadata for their IR might induce nausea in repository managers. Fortunately, our IMLS National Leadership Grant intends, as one of its deliverables, to help address this problem. OCLC is a partner in the grant and will develop crosswalks between Dublin Core and one or more of the publishing industry schemas recommended by GS. We also plan to develop automated transformation mechanisms to minimize the work required to express citation data more effectively for indexing. The products of that grant will be published in a toolkit around 2014 and will be hosted on the Digital Library Federation's website.

SUMMARY

Transforming IRs to GS-preferred metadata schemas is very likely to raise their indexing ratio.. We demonstrated that transforming Dublin Core metadata tags to Highwire Press tags increased the sample data set GS indexing ratio from 0 percent to 62 percent in the second pilot and achieved a 90 percent GS indexing ration after tripling the sample size from 19 to 56 papers in the third pilot. Transforming metadata to EPrints, PRISM, and bepress schemas are likely to have a similar effect.

The low indexing ratio of IRs in GS is widespread, and it cuts across institutions and repository software. Despite GS's endorsement of three software packages, our survey demonstrated that software is not a deciding factor for indexing ratio in GS. Each of the three recommended software packages showed reasonably good indexing ratios for some repositories and very poor ratios for others. Those repositories that followed GS recommendations for crawler indexing and metadata schemas were much more likely to achieve high indexing ratios.

While transforming metadata seems to be an effective route to getting indexed, individual IRs may have additional SEO-related problems that must be addressed as well. As we have indicated in earlier chapters, slow or misconfigured servers, failure to submit viable sitemaps, crawler errors that remain unresolved, failure to provide appropriate server response codes, lack of communication across the organization, and a host of other potential problems must be considered for effective SEO that will raise repositories' visibility in all search engine indexes. Advanced methods for optimizing PDF files may also help to assure inclusion in the GS index.

The growing use of GS by researchers underscores the need to address the problem of low IR indexing ratio, particularly as more emphasis is being placed on assessment and measurement of outputs. IRs have the potential to raise author citation rates and in turn to affect university rankings, but this potential may be seriously hampered if IR content is invisible to researchers who use GS.

Chapter Eight

Measuring Success

We cannot call a digital-library or electronic-publishing system a success if we cannot measure and interpret its use.
—Peterson Bishop, 1998

Communicating the use and performance of digital repositories has been an underlying theme of this book. Addressing SEO issues will have limited value if you're unable to show stakeholders the resulting improvements, so you'll want to provide them with reports and dashboard tools that enable them to monitor their interests. Be careful of the language you use. The archivist with intimate knowledge of the collection is unlikely to be interested in talking about how the "indexing ratio" of the collection in Google has improved. He will want to know how many people are viewing the collection and if those views are driving requests for more information. The institutional repository manager doesn't care so much if more papers have been harvested and indexed by Google Scholar; she will want data to show faculty that their papers are being downloaded and cited as a result, because that will help her promote the usefulness of the IR. The archivist and the IR manager are examples of stakeholders, and reporting mechanisms that measure the effectiveness of daily decisions will help them achieve their goals and gauge the value they are providing as they compete for funding and resources.

In this last chapter we'll talk in some detail about the specific factors that go into creating good reports that will be useful to different stakeholders. We'll first develop a conceptual model for measuring success, because that will help us understand what to measure and for whom. Metrics will vary for different stakeholders, and a high-level understanding of what drives each of those stakeholders will tell us what kind of data should be collected. Their audiences, in turn, motivate stakeholders.

Knowing what drives each of those groups is half the battle. It's one thing to set up Google Analytics and then watch the charts and graphs and poke into the numbers a bit, but that just amounts to floundering. Setting goals and measuring progress against them by using key performance indicators (KPIs) will achieve a level of evaluation that generates useful reports. The hard part of this process is identifying and prioritizing your stakeholders' goals. Setting up tools like Google Analytics to report appropriate metrics is the (relatively) easy part.

DEFINITIONS FOR MEASURING SUCCESS

The following list defines the terms that we will be using in this chapter. Some of these will be explained more specifically in later sections.

Stakeholder—an individual, team, or organization that has interests in the outcome of a program.

Examples: funding provider; content provider; collection manager

Driver—something that creates, motivates, and fuels change. Drivers are internal and external influences on high-level stakeholders who are responsible for setting organizational priorities, allocating money, directing resources, and so on.

Examples: digital access; demand for accountability

Goal—an end state that a stakeholder intends to achieve. Goals are generally expressed using qualitative words consistent with a stakeholder's position within an organizational hierarchy.

Examples:

improve website navigation to targeted items (IT Department)

increase College of Engineering IR visitor traffic (IR manager)

support scientific and engineering research programs (library funding provider)

Key Performance Indicators (KPIs)—measureable values of a particular activity. Each goal should have one or more KPIs as a measure of performance of the goal.

Examples: exit pages; bounce rate; traffic sources; and so on

Metric—quantifies the KPI.

Examples: social network referrals; page views; visitors

IDENTIFYING STAKEHOLDERS

Stakeholders for digital repositories tend to fall into three broad categories: funders, content providers, and organizational/operational support (i.e., staff, technology, and so on). These three stakeholders work together to reach intended users (or audience). Each stakeholder has a set of goals and expectations for the collection, and the collection manager should track progress toward each goal through selected metrics.

We have extended this outline to identify the basic characteristics that each digital repository shares:

- Funding providers
- Content providers
- Goals and objectives driven by stakeholders
- Target audience(s) determined by stakeholders
- Organizational and operational support
- Key performance indicators (KPIs) to evaluate "business performance"

This model can be applied to all digital repositories and is illustrated in figure 8.1, "Stakeholder Motivation."

Funders

People or organizations that fund digital repositories want to know that the money they're providing is having a positive effect, and formal funding agencies will want that measurement to begin during the proposal-writing stage. Funders want to know what problem their money will address, of course, but they're particularly interested in how many people will be affected, and how you are going to measure that impact. They may require you to use a formal evaluation methodology, such as outcome based evaluation (OBE) or balanced scorecard. OBE methodology relies on projections about how much improvement you expect to see in your target audience knowledge, or in how much better they will be able to perform some action as a result of your project. Pre- and post-evaluations can be helpful in

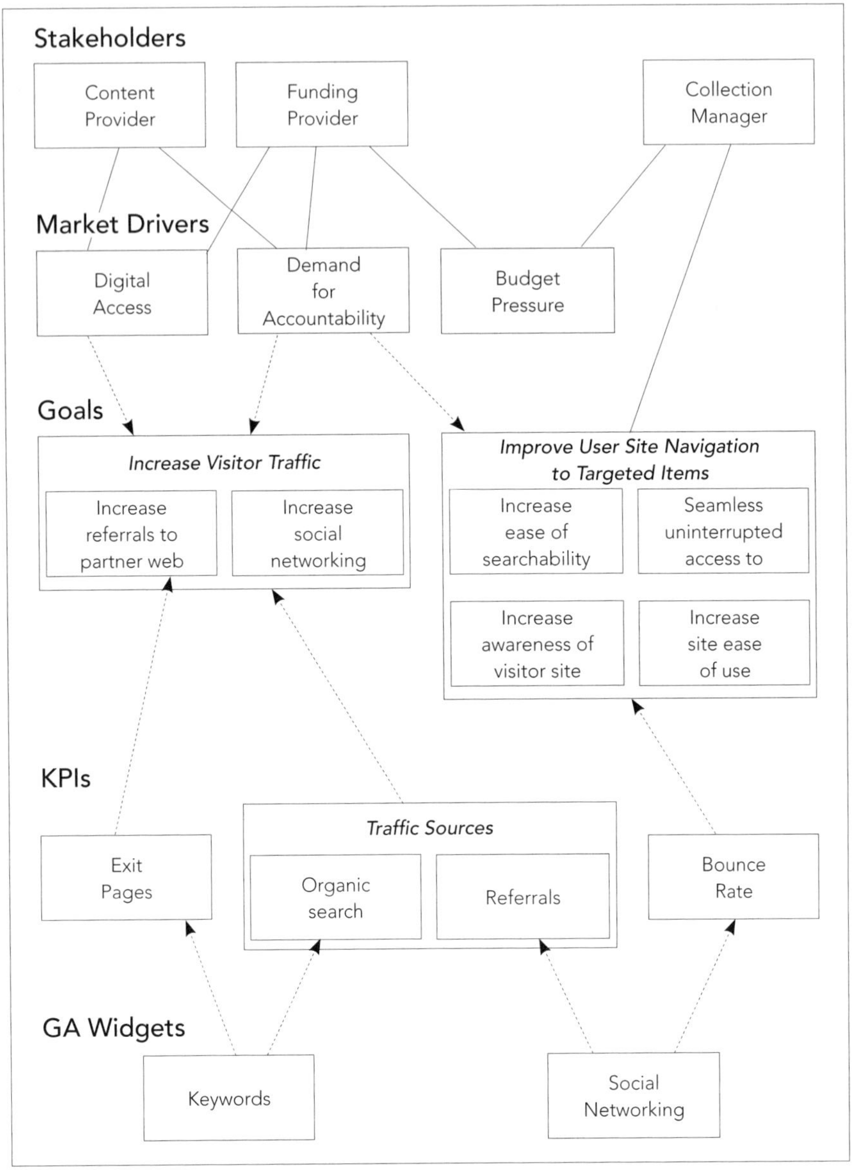

FIGURE 8.1
Motivation Example

determining this. Balanced scorecard measures performance from four perspectives: customers, learning and growth, internal business processes, and financial. It is considered "balanced" because it measures both financial and nonfinancial data (Ramage and Armstrong 2005).

Content Providers

Content providers are the donors, organizations, subject specialists, and archivists that contribute the digital objects that comprise a repository. In the case of IRs the content providers are usually the publication authors.

Organizational/Operational Support

The collection managers and any staff that contribute to the creation and maintenance of the repository make up the day-to-day support needed to achieve the collection's goals. This includes all the roles we identified in chapter 2. For the most part, these staff report up to executive administrators who are held accountable by funders and content providers.

The people in this group who have the most authority are the content experts, whose analog or existing digital materials are being used to provide the material content of the repository.

Audience (or Customer)

The collection audience is, of course, the real reason we create digital repositories, and their use (or lack of use) of the repository is of paramount importance to the funding and content providers. Given the increasing trend for accountability by funding and content providers, we believe it is critical that the collection managers and their supervisors define the repository's intended audience and determine how they plan to measure whether the repository is accessible and reaching the intended audience. Identifying the repository's audience early on helps align all the stakeholders in using the funding to get support in place and do the work necessary to bring the repository into existence. In academic settings audiences are usually subdivided into three categories—students, faculty, and staff—but don't forget the public community.

While it's easy to put tools in place to track digital repository usage, the challenge is ensuring the tools are aligned with the goals and objectives established with stakeholders. This requires that tracking tools provide content managers with insight on the efficiency and effectiveness of using organizational and operational support to reach the target audiences.

KNOW THE ENVIRONMENT AND WHAT'S DRIVING HIGH-LEVEL DECISIONS

Environmental factors set the stage for measuring success, and paying attention to the prognostications of national organizations can help align internal goals with external trends. The Research Planning and Review Committee of the Association of College and Research Libraries (ACRL), for instance, has identified at least three trends that are relevant to digital repository stakeholders.

Increasing Demands for Accountability and Demonstrated Value

Academic libraries are increasingly required to demonstrate the value they provide to their clientele and institutions (ACRL Research Planning and Review Committee 2010) and "librarians no longer can rely on their stakeholders' belief in their importance. Rather, they must demonstrate their value" (Association of College and Research Libraries and Oakleaf, Megan 2012)

Continuing Budget Pressures

Budget challenges will persist as endowments struggle to recover from the recent recession and education budgets remain stagnant or continue to be cut (ACRL Research Planning and Review Committee 2010). While academia has often been sheltered from the kind of economic realities faced by businesses, budgeting is increasingly tied to performance and perceived value.

Unknown Demand for Digitized Collection Items

Just as most libraries can no longer afford the "just-in-case" approach to collection development, the "build it and they will come" model of digitization is also no longer affordable. Digital repository managers must get better at using their limited resources to identify which items to digitize first and how to market them to achieve their goals. This becomes even more difficult as demands and expectations for speed, ease of use, and access are increasing along with the diversity of Internet devices being used to access digital collection content.

Like a museum curator, a digital collection manager cannot put everything he or she has on display for the public. The manager should invest time and resources in maximizing the metadata, links, and other SEO signals we have identified for each item they digitize. We believe it is better to have fewer items that perform well in search engines and lead users to your collections than having a lot of items that are buried in SERPs with low visibility and poor click-through. In this proposed scenario of fewer digitized objects being made available, the collection manager should select items that represent maximum diversity. Having a diverse set of items that perform well in SERPs should lead to more traffic and increased opportunity to start a dialogue about the other items contained in the collection that have not yet been digitized. For this reason it is important for the collection manager to think about incorporating tools that allow users to provide feedback and request more information.

ALIGNING PLANS WITH GOALS

The best place to start is by reviewing your organization's strategic plan and evaluating how it aligns with the strategic plans of major funding providers. Most funders don't want to waste their time reviewing proposals if their priorities are not addressed. Nearly all government-funding agencies also require post-funding evaluations that include the activities used to bring about change and the resulting outcomes. This may influence whether the applicant will be eligible for continued funding. Given these expectations, collection managers must understand funding providers' goals and develop outcome metrics that can be tracked on an ongoing basis and provided as a measure of their program's success, as well as highlighting areas that need attention and opportunities for expansion. Funding recipients must be prepared to track and measure progress throughout the funding period.

The Institute of Museum and Library Services (IMLS) is one of the most important sources of grant funding for libraries and museums. It has stated that the two most important reasons for evaluation are "to provide essential information for good decisions about priorities, deployment of resources, and program design, and; to help communicate the value of initiatives (whether these are programs, services, or organizations—like libraries and museums)" (Hildreth 2012). The

Museum and Library Services Act of 2010 (PL 111-340) calls on IMLS to take an active role in research and data collection and to advise the president and Congress on museum, library, and information services (Institute of Museum and Library Services 2010). IMLS is required to provide a strategic plan and has placed emphasis on the following:

- "Using performance information to lead, learn, and improve outcomes"
- "Communicating performance coherently and concisely for better results and transparency" (Institute of Museum and Library Services 2011)

The IMLS strategic plan states that "IMLS is focusing on areas where it can best effect change and measure its results." The IMLS assessment model (figure 8.2) will "identify effective museum and library services through performance monitoring" among other things (Institute of Museum and Library Services 2011).

IMLS is serious about using performance-based pre- and post-grant funding decisions, and we believe digital collection managers must look for ways to align and support the IMLS Strategic Plan, 2012–2016: Creating a Nation of Learners. The most obvious opportunity is Strategic Goal #3: "The IMLS supports exemplary stewardship of museum and library collections and promotes the use of technology to facilitate discovery of knowledge and cultural heritage." In particular:

Objective 3.1: "Support the care and management of the nation's collections, both material and living, to expand and sustain access for current and future generations."

Objective 3.2: "Develop and implement a nationwide strategy to expand public access to the information, meaning, and content found in museum and library collections."

While collection managers can demonstrate support for these objectives by providing metrics such as page views, visits, visitors, downloads, and so on, we believe the library community will be better served by including additional accessibility metrics such as:

- Number of digital items indexed by major search engines, (e.g., Google, Bing)
- References to collection content using tools like Article Level Metrics developed by PLoS (Public Library of Science 2009).

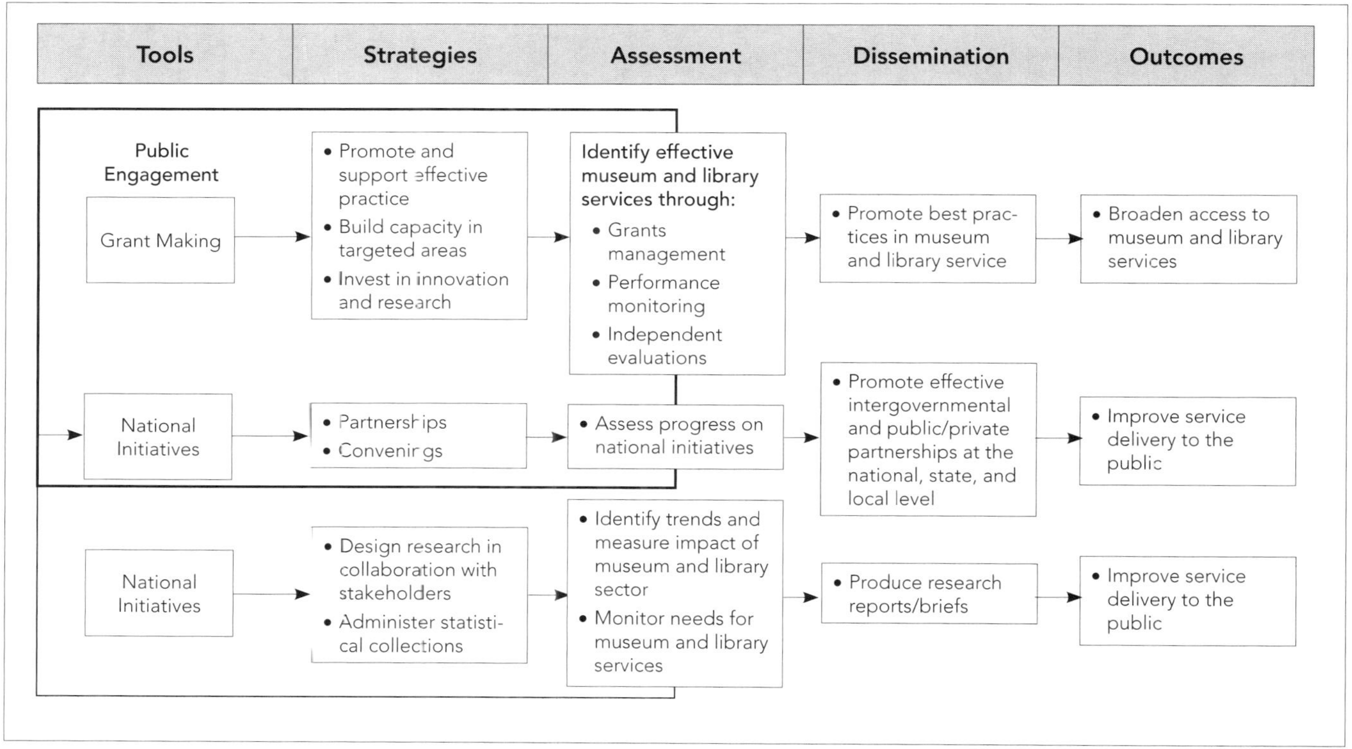

FIGURE 8.2
IMLS Performance Improvement Model

- PDF and bibliographic citation downloads from IR, by college and department
- Request for information about the collection

IMLS is just one funding agency that makes its funding priorities and evaluation criteria clear. Below are additional examples of how digital repositories can directly support some of the National Endowment for the Humanities' primary goals and objectives, based on the 2007–2012 NEH strategic plan:

- "To advance knowledge and understanding in the humanities in the United States."

  "Facilitate basic research and original scholarship in the humanities" might be supported by providing data on the visits and page views generated by users referred by academic search engines (e.g., Google Scholar), and downloads of IR collection content or bibliographic citations.

  "Strengthen teaching and learning in the humanities in elementary and secondary schools and higher educational institutions across the nation" can be measured by providing data on access and behavior of collection content by users with K–12 schools and higher education IP addresses.

- "To broaden public awareness of, access to, and support for the humanities."

  "Extend the reach of the humanities" can be demonstrated by providing data on the number of digital items indexed by major search engines (e.g., Google, Bing) and references to collection content using Article Level Metrics tools such as the PLoS ALM.

Library administrators and collection managers who clearly prioritize the goals and objectives of their funding and content providers will have better success gaining support for their digital repositories. To maintain long-term funding and support, they must also ensure KPIs are established and tools are in place to monitor progress on a weekly and monthly basis. They should actively review the information and ask questions to ensure their organization is aligned and focused on delivering the goals that have been established.

RELEVANT LIBRARY WEB METRICS

What visitors are viewing on the website, where they are spending their time, and how they access the website are influential in optimizing a website that supports stakeholders' goals and objectives. The key to website optimization is the analysis of the data you collect to make informed decisions on how to achieve goals and objectives with fewer resources in less time. The types of website analytics that digital collection managers should focus on include the following:

Visitor Behavior—Monitoring visitor behavior will include metrics such as page views, unique visitors, total visits, and average time spent on site. The goal of analyzing these metrics is to understand how often visitors come to the site and what lengths of time they are spending on the site.

Site Content—Site content will include metrics such as pages, site section views, and unique page views. The goal of analyzing these metrics is to understand what content visitors are viewing, downloading, and spending the most time consuming on the site.

Paths—Path metrics will include landing pages, exit pages, visitor flow, and bounce rates. The goal of analyzing site navigation paths is to understand what paths visitors take to reach and view the website.

Traffic Sources—Traffic sources for the website include search keywords, search engines, and referrals. The goal of analyzing site traffic sources is to understand where and how people are reaching the site.

Retention—Site visitor retention metrics include visitor frequency and recency, new vs. returning visitors, and visit number. The goal of analyzing visitor retention metrics is to understand the behavior of returning visitors and what they are doing when they return to the site.

Based upon discussions with digital repository managers, we have identified the KPIs that help answer common questions of managers and their stakeholders:

Why are users visiting the collection?

- Organic search keywords
- Internal search keywords

- Landing pages
- Site pages viewed

How are users getting to the collection?

- Organic search
- Social media
- Referrals
- Direct access

Who is using the site?

- Visitor location (country, state)
- Visitor demographic information (e.g., K–12, .edu, .com IP address)
- Domains linking to the collection (e.g., Wikipedia, .gov, .edu)

How many visitors and visits are the sites getting?

- Total visits by time period
- Daily visits
- New vs. return visits
- Return frequency
- Average time spent on site
- Number of pages viewed per visit

The number and types of downloads being generated by each collection

Key Performance Indicators

Listed below are some of the more common KPIs that are reported for website visitation.

Hits—An almost useless metric because it counts the number of files that are requested from a web server. Since every image on a page is a file, a single page view can indicate dozens or even hundreds of hits. If you hear anyone boast about how many "hits" their website gets, walk away. Either they don't know what they're talking about or their numbers are inflated.

Page Views—Far more useful than a hit, a page view represents the call and display of a complete page on your site.

Visits—Indicates a single user's visitation to your site, following that user as he navigates through specific pages on your site.

Session—Indicates the time spent by a user on your site, but ends when the user clicks off to another site.

Bounce Rate—Shows the percentage of users who visit a single page on your site and then leave. Bounce rate is not necessarily a bad thing, since it might indicate that the user found exactly what they were looking for on that single page.

Click Path—Tracks the navigation path the user takes through your site.

Click-Through Rate—The percentage of users that click a link after they view it. For example, the links on the first page of Google SERPs have a much higher click-though rate than the second page of SERPs.

Return Visitors—Also known as "loyalty," this metric distinguishes users who visit more than once from new users.

COLLECTING DATA: LOG FILES OR PAGE TAGGING?

Collecting data is the first step to providing meaningful reports, and there are two main options for data collection: log files and page tagging. Each method requires configuration for maximum effectiveness.

Log Files

Most systems administrators will know about standard log file data collection because log files are geared toward analysis of how well the server is performing. This method gathers a lot of very useful information that can help a systems administrator determine the load being placed on their server, whether the hardware is appropriate for that load, bandwidth use, and so on. It also tracks IP addresses of visitors, which are useful pieces of data but must be handled with care due to privacy concerns. The raw log files can be viewed and manipulated by a number of commercial and open source log file analytics software. However, log files are deficient for marketing purposes due to the difficulty of tracking users across domains or physical servers, or integrating marketing concepts such as event and goal tracking. Log files provide data about a physical server, and while one server

We recommend that digital collection systems administrators use the W3C's extended log file format (Hallam-Baker and Behlendorf). The changes are simple to make and provide more information with better control of the data that most analytics software can read (Jansen and Spink 2009).

can host multiple website domains, the default configuration for log files doesn't gather data across those domains. Most repository websites are complex, spanning multiple domains across multiple physical servers. Addressing this issue once again requires good communication so that the systems administrator configures the log files to collect useful information for various stakeholders. Systems administrators should also know how to configure log files appropriately for the web server software they're running—usually Apache or Windows IIS.

Page Tagging

Page tagging is the second method for data collection, and we talked briefly about this in chapter 4 when we discussed the configuration of Google Analytics. When you employ page tagging you put a little bit of code, usually JavaScript, on each page of your website that sets a cookie and calls an invisible image on your particular website analytics software's remote server. The software manages the collected data behind the scenes and displays it in attractive and useful ways. It's an easy method of data collection, and it can even be used by website administrators who have no administrative access to the servers, like in hosted environments. Page tagging is a very noninvasive way of gathering information about your visitors; it's considered "safe" and doesn't violate any privacy concerns. Google Analytics won't reveal the IP addresses, for instance, of your users.

This safety comes at a price, though. Because the page tagging data collection method utilizes cookies and JavaScript, users can defeat it by instructing their browsers not to allow cookies or JavaScript, or by telling browsers they do not wish to be tracked (Marek 2011). Another issue with page tagging is that without some fairly complex configuration it underreports access to non-HTML files, such as PDF or Word documents (.docx). As mentioned in the previous chapter, this is significant for IRs using page tagging because search engines that send user traffic directly to PDF documents, such as Google Scholar, are not captured because page tagging code requires the user vist an HTML page on your website first.

Clearly, neither method of data collection by itself will provide a complete picture, but combining log file and page-tagging practices creates a very robust

As part of our IMLS grant, we have partnered with the Digital Library Federation to create a community called "SEO for Digital Libraries." The community may be reached at the Council on Library and Information Resources (CLIR) website at

http://connect.clir.org/CLIR/Communities/ViewCommunities/ViewAllCommunities/

The community site includes tools to help collection managers using Google Analytics improve the accuracy of non-HTML file access and coss-domain tracking.

data set that can provide useful reports for a variety of internal and external stakeholders.

ELIMINATING NOISE

Key performance indicators do provide useful metrics, otherwise we wouldn't advocate monitoring them. But we'll also throw out a word of caution at this point. We tend to think of numbers as indicating precision, but the log file and page-tagging methods of data collection are not precise and that's an important fact to keep in mind. The data that you observe are most useful when you consider them to be directional and showing trends, so be patient and be prepared to observe the data over a period of time. Don't get caught up in details of small numbers, and don't make drastic changes to your repositories or websites based on small movements in the data. Decide which KPIs you need to look at on a daily, monthly, and weekly basis. Trying to interpret user behavior or performance data on a less than weekly basis is probably a waste of time unless you have a ton of traffic that generates over 100 data points per day for the metrics you want to evaluate. Even bounce rates will fluctuate over time.

We've mentioned before the importance of being able to gather data across domains, but it's worth stressing again. If your website and repository presence spans domains or subdomains—and most do at this point—your reports will be both incomplete and skewed if you aren't able to gather data accordingly. The institutions that can report this way will be able to show a more complete picture of use and performance of their repositories, and thus provide more insight into how best to allocate resources.

Another factor to keep in mind is the limitation of the SEO that most libraries and archives can afford. While we're confident that the practices we've outlined will help you significantly increase the use of your repositories, serious SEO is indeed a kind of rocket science and it costs a lot of money in personnel, expertise, and tools. We have advocated the use of Google Analytics in this book because it is sophisticated and free web analytics software, but it's nowhere near as sophisticated as the corporate business solutions provided by Google Analytics, Adobe Omniture, or Webtrends that cost tens of thousands of dollars annually. Most of us will never dream of having that kind of a budget for SEO.

COMMUNICATING RESULTS

The most obvious way to communicate results to stakeholders is with written reports. Many analytics packages allow you to produce reports that display your chosen metrics in colorful charts and graphs, and those visuals can be worked into projected presentations as well. A customized analytics dashboard is another very powerful reporting mechanism. A stakeholder who has immediate access to personalized repository metrics through Google Analytics, for instance, will have a heightened sense of control and appreciation, and will be able to generate his or her own reports as needed. The drawback, of course, is that the stakeholder may watch the numbers too closely and frequently may want IT staff to react to small changes in the reported metrics by making system-level adjustments. It's useful to convey that the numbers are indicative and should be viewed as trends over longer periods of time.

SUMMARY

Measuring the results of SEO practice is important to communicating the success of your work. Reports can demonstrate which SEO practices are working and which need attention or improvement. More important, reports will demonstrate to stakeholders that the digital repositories are being used and that the funding and other resources are justified. Stakeholders can be external (funders and donors) or internal (collection managers and administrators) and always have a target audience that motivates and influences their decision making. In order to accurately measure results you must first understand the needs and wants of your stakeholders. What drives them? What goals do they want to achieve with their digital repositories? How do they measure success?

Don't be afraid to show numbers associated with your starting point. Our baseline SEO metrics were frighteningly low, but they made later successes appear even more dramatic. Imagine being able to show an indexing ratio for a given collection going from 2 percent to 80 percent in less than a year, and then also being able to show that search engine referrals for all collections doubled in the same period, and that visitation increased by more than 80 percent. Numbers like that make an impact and have a way of quieting stakeholder complaints almost overnight.

References

ACRL Research Planning and Review Committee. 2010. "2010 Top Ten Trends in Academic Libraries: A Review of the Current Literature." *College & Research Libraries News* 71, no. 6 (June 1): 286–92.

Alpert, Jesse, and Nissan Hajaj. 2008. "We Knew the Web Was Big. . ." *Official Google Blog*. http://googleblog.blogspot.com/2008/07/we-knew-web-was-big.html.

Angotti, David. 2011. "Will Google Plus Put Facebook Out of Business?" *Search Engine Journal*. http://www.searchenginejournal.com/facebook-google-plus-growth/38337/.

———. 2012. "Google Chrome Penalized for Violating Quality Guidelines." *Search Engine Journal*. http://www.searchenginejournal.com/google-penalizes-chrome/38469/.

Assisi, Francis C. 2005. "Anurag Acharya Helped Google's Scholarly Leap." *INDOlink - Science & Technology*. http://www.indolink.com/SciTech/fr010305-075445.php.

Association of College and Research Libraries, and Megan Oakleaf. 2012. *Value of Academic Libraries: A Comprehensive Research Review and Report*. Chicago: Association of College and Research Libraries. http://www.acrl.ala.org/value/.

Autocrat. 2009. "The Number of Pages/URLs in the SERPs/GWMT/Sitemaps Decreasing/Going Down/Fluctuating/Don't Match." *Google Webmaster Central Help Forum*. http://www.google.com/support/forum/p/Webmasters/thread?tid=12785ecb88b7436d&hl=en.

Baty, Phil. 2011. "Change for the Better." *The Times Higher Education: World University Rankings 2011–12*, October 6. http://www.timeshighereducation.co.uk/world-university-rankings/2011-2012/analysis-rankings-methodology.html.

Bing. 2009. "Webmaster Tools." *Bing*. http://www.bing.com/toolbox/webmaster.

Brin, Sergey, and Lawrence Page. 1998. "The Anatomy of a Search Engine." http://infolab.stanford.edu/~backrub/google.html.

Britton, Evan. 2011. "4 Ways to Utilize the Google Keyword Tool." *Business Insider*. http://www.businessinsider.com/4-ways-to-utilize-the-google-keyword-tool-2011-6.

Brutlag, Jake. 2009. "Speed Matters." *Google Research Blog*. http://googleresearch.blogspot.com/2009/06/speed-matters.html.

comScore. 2012. “comScore Releases March 2012 U.S. Search Engine Rankings.” Press releases. *comScore.* http://www.comscore.com/Press_Events/Press_Releases/2012/4/comScore_Releases_March_2012_U.S._Search_Engine_Rankings.

Cutts, Matt. 2007. “Subdomains and Subdirectories.” *Matt Cutts: Gadgets, Google, and SEO.* http://www.mattcutts.com/blog/subdomains-and-subdirectories/.

———. 2010a. “How Search Works.” *You Tube.* http://www.youtube.com/watch?v=BNHR6IQJGZs.

———. 2010b. “Does Google Use Data from Social Sites in Ranking?” *You Tube - GoogleWebmasterHelp.* http://www.youtube.com/watch?v=ofhwPC-5Ub4&noredirect=1.

———. 2012. “Another Step to Reward High-Quality Sites.” *Google Webmaster Central Blog.* http://googlewebmastercentral.blogspot.com/2012/04/another-step-to-reward-high-quality.html.

danbri. 2011. “Using RDFa 1.1 Lite with Schema.org.” *Schema Blog.* http://blog.schema.org/2011/11/using-rdfa-11-lite-with-schemaorg.html.

DCMI. 2005. “Guidelines for Encoding Bibliographic Citation Information in Dublin Core Metadata.” *Dublin Core Metadata Initiative.* http://dublincore.org/documents/dc-citation-guidelines/.

De Rosa, Cathy, Joanne Cantrell, Matthew Carlson, Peggy Gallagher, Janet Hawk, and Charlotte Sturtz. 2011. *Perceptions of Libraries, 2010: Context and Community: A Report to the OCLC Membership.* Ed. Brad Gauder. Dublin, Ohio: (OCLC) Online Computer Library Center. http://www.oclc.org/reports/2010perceptions/2010perceptions_all_singlepage.pdf.

De Rosa, Cathy, Joanne Cantrell, Diane Cellentani, Janet Hawk, Lillie Jenkins, and Alane Wilson. 2005. *Perceptions of Libraries and Information Resources: A Report to the OCLC Membership.* Dublin, Ohio: (OCLC) Online Computer Library Center. http://www.oclc.org/reports/pdfs/Percept_all.pdf.

Enge, Eric. 2010. “Eric Enge Interviews Matt Cutts.” *Stone Temple.* http://www.stonetemple.com/articles/interview-matt-cutts-012510.shtml.

Fishkin, Rand, and Bill Tancer. 2009a. “Figure 6.1 - Search Engine Keyword Demand.” *SEOmoz.* http://www.seomoz.org/img/upload/search-demand-curve.gif.

———. 2009b. “Figure 6.2 - The Search Demand Curve.” *SEOmoz.* http://www.seomoz.org/img/upload/search-demand-curve%281%29.gif.

———. 2009c. “Figure 6.3 - The Search Demand Curve, Competition & Conversion.” *SEOmoz.* http://www.seomoz.org/img/upload/search-demand-features.gif.

Fox, Vanessa. 2009. “Google Search Now Supports Microformats and Adds ‘Rich Snippets’ to Search Results.” *Search Engine Land.* http://searchengineland.com/google-search-now-supports-microformats-and-adds-rich-snippets-to-search-results-19055.

———. 2011. "Schema.org: Google, Bing & Yahoo Unite to Make Search Listings Richer through Structured Data." *Search Engine Land.* http://searchengineland.com/schema-org-google-bing-yahoo-unite-79554.

———. 2012. "Google's Upcoming Algorithm Change: 'Overly-Optimized Sites.'" *Nine by Blue.* http://www.ninebyblue.com/google-optimized/.

Goel, Kavi, and Pravir Gupta. 2011. "Introducing Schema.org: Search Engines Come Together for a Richer Web." *Official Google Blog.* http://googleblog.blogspot.com/2011/06/introducing-schemaorg-search-engines.html.

Goodman, Eli, and James Green. 2012. "Beyond Search Engines: The Brave New World of Retargeting Data." PDF presented at the comScore Webinar, March 28. http://www.comscore.com/Press_Events/Presentations_Whitepapers/2012/Beyond_Search_Engines_The_Brave_New_World_of_Retargeting_Data.

Google. 1998. "Company Corporate Information." http://www.google.com/about/corporate/company/.

———. 2010. "Google Webmaster Central." http://www.google.com/webmasters/.

———. 2011a. "About Site Verification." *Google Webmaster Tools Help.* http://www.google.com/support/webmasters/bin/answer.py?hl=en&answer=35179.

———. 2011b. "Creating Useful 404 Pages." *Google Webmaster Tools Help.* http://support.google.com/webmasters/bin/answer.py?hl=en&answer=93641.

———. 2011c. "Multiple Users." *Google Webmaster Tools Help.* https://www.google.com/support/webmasters/bin/answer.py?answer=44227&hl=en.

———. 2011d. "My Site Isn't Doing Well in Search." *Google Webmaster Tools Help.* http://www.google.com/support/webmasters/bin/answer.py?hl=en&answer=34444&from=34443&rd=1.

———. 2011e. "Rel='nofollow'." *Google Webmaster Tools Help.* http://support.google.com/webmasters/bin/answer.py?hl=en&answer=96569.

———. 2011f. "Google Basics." *Google Webmaster Tools Help.* http://support.google.com/webmasters/bin/answer.py?hl=en&answer=70897.

———. 2011g. "About Rel='canonical'." *Google Webmaster Tools Help.* http://support.google.com/webmasters/bin/answer.py?hl=en&answer=139394.

———. 2012a. "Google AdWords: Keyword Tool." *Google AdWords.* https://adwords.google.com/select/KeywordToolExternal?defaultView=2.

———. 2012b. "URLs Restricted by Robots.txt Errors." *Google Webmaster Tools Help.* http://support.google.com/webmasters/bin/answer.py?hl=en&answer=35235.

———. 2012c."Event Tracking Guide - Google Analytics." *Google Developers.* https://developers.google.com/analytics/devguides/collection/gajs/eventTrackerGuide.

———. 2012d. "Page Speed Family." *Google Code.* http://code.google.com/speed/page-speed/docs/overview.html.

Google Scholar. 2011a. "Indexing Guidelines." Inclusion Guidelines. *About Google Scholar.* http://scholar.google.com/intl/en/scholar/inclusion.html#indexing.

———. 2011b. "Inclusion Guidelines for Webmasters." Inclusion Guidelines. *About Google Scholar.* http://scholar.google.com/intl/en/scholar/inclusion.html.

Grimes, Carrie. 2010. "Our New Search Index: Caffeine." *Official Google Blog.* http://googleblog.blogspot.com/2010/06/our-new-search-index-caffeine.html.

Hagans, Andy. 2005. "High Accessibility Is Effective Search Engine Optimization." *A List Apart,* November 8. http://www.alistapart.com/articles/accessibilityseo.

Haglund, Lotta, and Per Olsson. 2008. "The Impact on University Libraries of Changes in Information Behavior among Academic Researchers: A Multiple Case Study." *Journal of Academic Librarianship* 34, no. 1 (January): 52–59.

Hallam-Baker, Phillip M., and Brian Behlendorf. "Extended Log File Format." *W3C.* http://www.w3.org/TR/WD-logfile.html.

Hamasu, Claire, and John Bramble. 2012. "The Medium Defines the Message." Conference presentation at the Utah Library Association Annual Conference, April 26, Salt Lake City, Utah. http://conference.ula.org/sites/conference.ula.org/files/SocialMedia_Hamasu-Bramble.pdf.

Herrera, Gail. 2010. "Google Scholar Users & User Behaviors: An Exploratory Study." *College & Research Libraries* (July 23). http://crl.acrl.org/content/early/2010/07/23/crl-125rl.abstract.

Hickson, Ian. 2011. "HTML Microdata." *W3C.* http://www.w3.org/TR/microdata/.

Hildreth, Susan. 2012. "Grant Applications / Outcome Based Evaluation / Purposes." *Institute of Museum and Library Services.* http://www.imls.gov/applicants/purposes.aspx.

Honen, Tomer, and Kaspar Szymanski. 2011. "How to Deal with Planned Site Downtime." *Official Google Webmaster Central Blog.* http://googlewebmastercentral.blogspot.com/2011/01/how-to-deal-with-planned-site-downtime.html.

Ingram, Mathew. 2010. "Is Facebook's Social Search Engine a Google Killer?" *Gigaom.* http://gigaom.com/2010/06/25/is-facebooks-social-search-engine-a-google-killer/.

Institute of Museum and Library Services. 2010. "IMLS Legislative Timeline." *Institute of Museum and Library Services / About Us / Legislation & Budget.* http://www.imls.gov/about/imls_legislative_timeline.aspx.

———. 2011. "Creating a Nation of Learners; IMLS Five-Year Strategic Plan 2012–2016." December 2. http://www.imls.gov/assets/1/AssetManager/StrategicPlan2012-16_Presentation.pdf.

Jackson, Mark. 2010. "Track XML or Server-Side PHP Files Using Google Analytics without JavaScript." *Mjdigital.* http://www.mjdigital.co.uk/blog/track-xml-or-server-side-files-using-google-analytics/.

Jansen, Bernard J., and Amanda Spink. 2009. *Handbook of Research on Web Log Analysis.* Hershey, PA: Information Science Reference, Idea Group Inc. (IGI). http://books

.google.com/books?id=db7YGbmADPUC&lpg=PT172&ots=N6IpEq6oJu&dq=benefits%20of%20extended%20log%20file&pg=PT172#v=onepage&q&f=false.

Key Perspectives Ltd., and Sheridan Brown. 2009. *A Comparative Review of Research Assessment Regimes in Five Countries and the Role of Libraries in the Research Assessment Process: A Pilot Study Commissioned by OCLC Research*. Dublin, Ohio: OCLC Research.

Keyword Discovery. 2011. "Keyword Usage Statistics on the Average Number of Keywords per Search Phrase by Country." *KeywordDiscovery.com*. http://www.keyworddiscovery.com/keyword-stats.html?date=2011-12-01.

Kitt, Denise. 2012. "Social Media Market Share Predictions for 2012." *MediaFunnel*. http://mediafunnel.com/social-media/social-media-market-share-2012/.

Koster, Martijn. 2010. "A Standard for Robot Exclusion." *Robotstxt.org*. http://www.robotstxt.org/orig.html#status.

Kroll, Susan, Rick Forsman, and OCLC Research. 2010. *A Slice of Research Life: Information Support for Research in the United States*. Dublin, Ohio: OCLC Research. http://www.oclc.org/research/publications/library/2010/2010-15.pdf.

Kunder, Maurice de. 2011. "The Size of the World Wide Web (The Internet)." *WorldWideWebSize.com*. http://www.worldwidewebsize.com/.

LaRock, Thomas. 2010. "Statistical Sampling for Verifying Database Backups." *Simple-talk*. http://www.simple-talk.com/sql/database-administration/statistical-sampling-for-verifying-database-backups/.

Lieb, Rebecca. 2009. *The Truth about Search Engine Optimization*. Upper Saddle River, NJ: FT. http://my.safaribooksonline.com/book/web-development/seo/9780768687873/write-for-users-and-search-engines-will-follow/42.

Marek, Kate. 2011. *Using Web Analytics in the Library*. Vol. 5. ALA Editions 47. ALA TechSource. http://books.google.com/books?id=sSnttrEXlDIC&pg=PA12&lpg=PA12&dq=page+tagging+turning+off+cookies&source=bl&ots=qC0j6V9mqw&sig=jI4rV3ZE6EnkRpjwyC8W7SnA3-w&hl=en&sa=X&ei=w4Z3T5iCK-egiQKp3aGoDg&ved=0CCoQ6AEwAQ#v=onepage&q=page%20tagging%20turning%20off%20cookies&f=false.

McGee, Matt. 2010a. "By the Numbers: Twitter vs. Facebook vs. Google Buzz." *Search Engine Land*. http://searchengineland.com/by-the-numbers-twitter-vs-facebook-vs-google-buzz-36709.

———. 2010b. "Facebook Passes Google (Again) as Most-Visited US Site: Hitwise." *Search Engine Land*. http://searchengineland.com/facebook-passes-google-again-as-most-visited-us-site-hitwise-38164.

McKay, Dana. 2007. "Institutional Repositories and Their 'Other' Users: Usability beyond Authors." *Ariadne* 52 (July). http://www.ariadne.ac.uk/issue52/mckay/.

Meho, Lokman I., and Kiduk Yang. 2007. "Impact of Data Sources on Citation Counts and Rankings of LIS Faculty: Web of Science Versus Scopus and Google Scholar."

Journal of the American Society for Information Science and Technology 58, no. 13 (November): 2105–25.

Mikki, Susanne. 2009. "Google Scholar Compared to Web of Science: A Literature Review." *Nordic Journal of Information Literacy in Higher Education* 1, no. 1: 41–51.

Miller, Rich. 2011. "Report: Google Uses about 900,000 Servers." *Data Center Knowledge.* http://www.datacenterknowledge.com/archives/2011/08/01/report-google-uses-about-900000-servers/.

Moskwa, Susan. 2011. "Do 404s Hurt My Site?" *Official Google Webmaster Central Blog.* http://googlewebmastercentral.blogspot.com/2011/05/do-404s-hurt-my-site.html.

Mueller, John. 2008. "Retiring Support for OAI-PMH in Sitemaps." *Official Google Webmaster Central Blog.* http://googlewebmastercentral.blogspot.com/2008/04/retiring-support-for-oai-pmh-in.html.

NetLingo. 2007. "Link Juice." *NetLingo: The Internet Dictionary.* http://www.netlingo.com/word/link-juice.php.

OCLC, Inc. 2012. "OCLC Adds Linked Data to WorldCat.org." *OCLC.* http://www.oclc.org/news/releases/2012/201238.htm.

Ohye, Maile. 2008. "More on 404." *Official Google Webmaster Central Blog.* http://googlewebmastercentral.blogspot.com/2008/08/now-that-weve-bid-farewell-to-soft-404s.html.

Page, Lawrence, Sergey Brin, Rajeev Motwani, and Terry Winograd. 1998. "The PageRank Citation Ranking: Bringing Order to the Web." Stanford University. Stanford InfoLab Publication Server. http://ilpubs.stanford.edu:8090/422/.

Peterson Bishop, Ann. 1998. "Logins and Bailouts: Measuring Access, Use, and Success in Digital Libraries." *Journal of Electronic Publishing* 4, no. 2 (December). doi:http://dx.doi.org/10.3998/3336451.0004.207. http://quod.lib.umich.edu/cgi/t/text/text-idx?c=jep;view=text;rgn=main;idno=3336451.0004.207.

Pingdom. 2008. "Map of All Google Data Center Locations." *Pingdom.* http://royal.pingdom.com/2008/04/11/map-of-all-google-data-center-locations/.

———. 2012. "Internet 2011 in Numbers." *Pingdom.* http://royal.pingdom.com/2012/01/17/internet-2011-in-numbers/.

Piwowar, Heather A., Roger S. Day, and Douglas B. Fridsma. 2007. "Sharing Detailed Research Data Is Associated with Increased Citation Rate." Ed. John Ioannidis. *PLoS ONE* 2, no. 3 (March 21): e308.

Public Library of Science (PLoS). 2009. "Article Level Metrics." *Public Library of Science (PLoS) Article Level Metrics.* http://article-level-metrics.plos.org/.

Ramage, Paul, and Anona Armstrong. 2005. "Measuring Success: Factors Impacting on the Implementation and Use of Performance Measurement within Victoria's Human Services Agencies." *Evaluation Journal of Australasia* 5, no. 2: 5–17.

Rieger, Oya Y. 2009. "Search Engine Use Behavior of Students and Faculty: User Perceptions and Implications for Future Research." *First Monday* 14, no. 12 (December 7). http://firstmonday.org/htbin/cgiwrap/bin/ojs/index.php/fm/article/view/2716/2385.

Ross, Jeanne W., and Peter Weill. 2002. "Six IT Decisions Your IT People Shouldn't Make." *Harvard Business Review* 80, no. 11. OnPoint Article (November): 84–95.

Schmidt, Eric. 2005. "Technology Is Making Marketing Accountable." Press Center speech transcript presented at the Association of National Advertisers, October 8. http://www.google.com/press/podium/ana.html.

Schonfeld, Roger C., and Ross Housewright. 2010. *Faculty Survey 2009: Key Insights for Libraries, Publishers, and Societies*. New York: Ithaka S+R. http://www.sr.ithaka.org/research-publications/faculty-survey-2009.

Schwartz, Barry. 2012a. "Matt Cutts: Google Update to Target Overly SEO'ed Web Sites in Upcoming Weeks." *Search Engine Roundtable*. http://www.seroundtable.com/google-over-seo-update-14887.html.

———. 2012b. "Google Over Optimization Launched, Google Names It Webspam Algorithm." *Search Engine Roundtable*. http://www.seroundtable.com/google-webspam-algorithm-15062.html.

———. 2012c. "Google Names the Over Optimization Penalty The Penguin Update." *Search Engine Roundtable*. http://www.seroundtable.com/google-penguin-update-15069.html.

Segal, David. 2011. "Search Optimization and Its Dirty Little Secrets." *The New York Times*, February 12, sec. Business Day. http://www.nytimes.com/2011/02/13/business/13search.html?_r=1.

Sernovitz, Andy. 2007. "How Companies Can Fix a Wikipedia Entry." *Damn, I Wish I'd Thought of That!* http://www.damniwish.com/how-companies-c/.

SEW Staff. 2007. "How to Use HTML Meta Tags." *Search Engine Watch (SEW)*. http://searchenginewatch.com/article/2067564/How-To-Use-HTML-Meta-Tags.

Singhal, Amit, and Matt Cutts. 2010. "Using Site Speed in Web Search Ranking." *Official Google Webmaster Central Blog*. http://googlewebmastercentral.blogspot.com/2010/04/using-site-speed-in-web-search-ranking.html.

sitemaps.org. 2008. "What Are Sitemaps?" *Sitemaps.org*. http://www.sitemaps.org/.

Stamoulis, Nick. 2010. "A Breakdown of the Google Webmaster Guidelines." *Search Engine Optimization Journal*. http://www.searchengineoptimizationjournal.com/google-webmaster-guidelines/.

Svore, Krysta M., Qiang Wu, Chris J. C. Burges, and Aaswath Raman. 2007. "Improving Web Spam Classification Using Rank-Time Features." In *Proceedings of the 3rd International Workshop on Adversarial Information Retrieval on the Web - AIRWeb '07, 9*, Banff, Alberta, Canada. http://portal.acm.org/citation.cfm?doid=1244408.1244411.

Tancer, Bill. 2008. "Sizing Up the Long Tail of Search." *Experian Hitwise Intelligence.* http://weblogs.hitwise.com/bill-tancer/2008/11/sizing_up_the_long_tail_of_sea.html.

Tatham, Matt. 2011. "Experian Hitwise Reports Bing-Powered Share of Searches at 29 Percent in August 2011." *Experian Hitwise.* http://press.experian.com/United-States/Press-Release/experian-hitwise-reports-bing-powered-share-of-searches-at-29-percent-in-august-2011.aspx?&p=1.

Theurer, Tenni. 2006. "Performance Research, Part 1: What the 80/20 Rule Tells Us about Reducing HTTP Requests." *Yahoo! User Interface Blog (YUIBlog).* http://yuiblog.com/blog/2006/11/28/performance-research-part-1/.

Times Higher Education. 2010. "The Times Higher Education World University Rankings 2010–2011." http://www.timeshighereducation.co.uk/world-university-rankings/.

University of Nottingham. 2011. "OpenDOAR - Home Page - Directory of Open Access Repositories." *OpenDOAR.* http://opendoar.org/.

Wikipedia. 2011. "Spider Trap - Wikipedia, the Free Encyclopedia." *Wikipedia.* http://en.wikipedia.org/wiki/Spider_trap.

———. 2012. "Keyword Stuffing." *Wikipedia.* http://en.wikipedia.org/wiki/Keyword_stuffing.

Yahoo! "Best Practices for Speeding Up Your Web Site." *Yahoo! Developer Network.* http://developer.yahoo.com/performance/rules.html.

About the Authors

Kenning Arlitsch

Kenning Arlitsch is the dean of the library at Montana State University. Prior to his current position he was the associate dean for information technology services at the University of Utah's J. Willard Marriott Library. He is the founder of the Mountain West Digital Library and the Utah Digital Newspapers program, as well as cofounder of the Western Waters Digital Library and the Western Soundscape Archive. Arlitsch holds an MLIS degree from the University of Wisconsin-Milwaukee, and a BA in English from Alfred University in New York. His current research is on search engine optimization for digital repositories, and he and his research partner, Patrick OBrien, have presented and published widely on the topic.

Patrick S. OBrien

Patrick S. OBrien is the semantic web research director at the Montana State University Library. Prior to his current position he was the SEO research manager at the University of Utah's J. Willard Marriott Library. He is an expert in semantic web technologies and their application for improving data integration quality, discovering new relationships, and turning diverse data stores into conceptual knowledge. OBrien has over fifteen years of experience implementing data-driven marketing and risk management strategy within various industries. His current research is on search engine optimization for digital repositories, and he and his research partner, Kenning Arlitsch, have presented and published widely on the topic. OBrien holds a BA in economics from UCLA and an MBA in marketing and finance from the University of Chicago Booth School of Business.

Index

T